WHO'S LISTENING?

LEONARD E. READ

WHO'S
LISTENING?

The Foundation for Economic Education, Inc.
Irvington-on-Hudson, New York 10533

ABOUT THE PUBLISHER

The Foundation for Economic Education is a non-political, nonprofit, educational institution. Its senior staff and numerous writers are students as well as teachers of the free market, private ownership, limited government rationale. Sample copies of the Foundation's monthly study journal, *The Freeman,* are available on request.

Published May 1973

(paper) ISBN-0-910614-47-4
(cloth) ISBN-0-910614-48-2

ABOUT THE AUTHOR

LEONARD READ was born on a farm in Michigan. Having the background of a 102-hour work week from 11 to 18, he maintains that "economic progress, not law, has lessened child labor." However, he looks back upon those early years, not as "child labor," but as a wonderful opportunity for growth.

At 19, his formal education was interrupted when he joined the Aviation Section of the Signal Corps. Following his service in England, France, and Germany during World War I, he sold insurance, worked as a cashier, then opened his own wholesale produce business. In 1927 he began a career in chamber of commerce work as secretary of a small organization. He then served for ten years as manager of the National Chamber's Western Division and, in 1939, became the General Manager of the Los Angeles Chamber, the largest of them all. In 1945 he was named Executive Vicepresident of the National Industrial Conference Board. He left the NICB in 1946 to organize and to become President of The Foundation for Economic Education, Inc.

Leonard Read is one of the founders of the Mont Pelerin Society. As a spokesman of the freedom philosophy, he has lectured widely throughout this country and abroad.

Besides numerous magazine articles in *The Freeman* and elsewhere in the American and foreign press, his works include the following books:

> Romance of Reality (o.p.)
> Pattern for Revolt
> Instead of Violence
> Outlook for Freedom (o.p.)
> Government: An Ideal Concept
> *Governo Um Concito Ideal*

Why Not Try Freedom?
  ¿Por Que No Ensayar la Libertad?
Elements of Libertarian Leadership
Anything That's Peaceful
  Todo Por la Paz
The Free Market and Its Enemy
  El Enemigo del Mercado Libre
Deeper Than You Think
Accent on the Right
The Coming Aristocracy
Let Freedom Reign
Talking to Myself
Then Truth Will Out
To Free or Freeze

To

One Who Listens

CONTENTS

Let me live in a house by the side of the road
   Where the race of men go by—
The men who are good and the men who are bad,
   As good and bad as I.
I would not sit in the scorner's seat
   Or hurl the cynic's ban—
Let me live in a house by the side of the road
   And be a friend to man.

—Sam Walter Foss

1

WHO'S LISTENING? I AM!

He who has ears to hear, let him hear.

—MARK 4:9

A devotee of the freedom philosophy, who rates highly the works of FEE, concludes a recent letter with a question that reveals discouragement: "But, who's listening?" Were his mood strictly the exception, I would let the matter pass. But, discouragement is disastrous. It is a foe of creative thinking. To accent the positive, to advance what's right—our task—requires an opposite mood: exuberance! A harmonious society can be brought about only by joyous people, never by those who are distraught. Anyway, I have an ancient and near-forgotten remedy for dejection; at least it works for me.

In answer to the question, who's listening to FEE, there are not millions, to be sure, but there are thousands. Audience size, however, is definitely not the proper criterion for measuring anyone's success. It is not who is listening to you or me but, rather, *are you and I listening*.

Were the number who listen to you or me the way to gauge

achievement, then we should emulate some celebrated political quack rather than the Lord. The demagogue—pick him yourself—has the more listeners, that is, if I am any good at counting noses.

Assume each and every person to be fretting about who is listening to his "words of wisdom." Now wave a magic wand that would, all of a sudden, make you alone a thousand times wiser. Result? No one would be wise enough to listen to you —a single sayer and no hearers! Clearly, this is not the way to spread wisdom.

Reflect on a better way that is all but forgotten. Let us listen for as much truth and righteousness as we can bring within earshot. Result? More than likely a thousand of us would be a thousand times wiser! In this case we would be listening to each other, each a stepping-stone for others—a human stairway ascending to wisdom.

The popular and erroneous way must lead to discouragement because so few ever listen. The way that seems right to me leads to encouragement simply because exuberance always attends intellectual and spiritual growth.

A fable comes to mind. The Sunday school teacher asked the little boy, "Who made you?" He replied, "Well, look at it this way, I am not finished yet." Who *is* finished? Not even the teacher, any more than the little boy! Life's purpose, if seen aright, is growth—each listening for wisdom—now and forever.

Each of us is in the making, and our making is aided and abetted if we fully grasp how interrelated we are, that is, if we recognize that each is at once an individualistic and a social being. Here is one way of phrasing it:

I am an I to me and You are an I to You. You are a You to me and I a You to You. In a word, all of us are at once I's and You's. This is to say that all the people on this earth—all the I's and all the You's—are interrelated. We are brethren, for good or ill, regardless of anyone's wishes in the matter. For better or for worse, every I among us has an impact on each of the You's—and vice versa. The I's and You's can be likened to an interconnected system of power stations—a grid —that distributes electricity over a large area, the performance of each station having a bearing on the whole system. Undeniably, we live in a "shared world."

In such a world intelligent attention to the I is the single way of being attentive to the well-being of all the You's. Elevation of the I is the sole means of sharing *beneficially*. By listening I learned:

> Our duties towards ourselves and towards our social environment coincide. Indeed, there is only one duty, namely: to grow mature.[1]

No You is upgraded except as some I grows in wisdom, and it is our good fortune that this is the way things are.

EDUCATION AN IN-TAKING PROCESS

Listening to the truth always has fortunate results. What does my listening reveal? That learning the truth or spreading wisdom—education—is now and forever an in-taking, never an out-bursting procedure. It may be possible for me to see

---

[1]Fritz Kunkel, *In Search of Maturity,* New York, 1943, p. 191.

your light; you cannot insinuate your enlightenment into me or anyone else.

Were the improvement of our social environment dependent on your or my "straightening out" those we believe to be short of understanding, the attempts would be utterly fruitless, the projects hopeless. Proof? Reflect on how impossible it is for me to cast you in my image or vice versa. Criticism is rarely packaged in a way that attracts customers.

The improvement of our social environment! That we are in trouble and plunging ever deeper is obvious to any perceptive person. If I were bent on socialism—authoritarianism by whatever name—I would encourage the current method in education, be it of the formal or informal kind, that is, the be-like-me or carbon-copy brand. Why? Because to the extent it is practiced, to that extent will no one, teacher or student, reformer or intended object, improve his thinking or his being. Down the drain unknowingly! Thus, correct methodology must be the first and foremost consideration of anyone interested in a good social environment.

SOMETHING WORTH TAKING

Once we realize that education is a taking-in process, we can then readily see that this presupposes that someone possesses something worth taking in. Nothing can be extracted from zeros. Is it not therefore fortunate that all we can do, indeed, all that we need to do to improve the social environment, is to "grow mature"? How? Listening!

Merely bear in mind that we are dealing with thinking, and thought is fragile. Thoughts are spiritual and not material;

they can only be inhaled, so to speak, and can no more be rammed into anyone's head than can a dream. The single way to "inhale" thoughts is to listen. "He who has ears to hear, let him hear."

There are two distinctly different sources to which the listener must attend: the Voices Without and also the Voice Within.

Listening to the Voices Without is an art demanding a rare quality of discrimination: the ability to distinguish between nonsense and wisdom.

Nonsense comes thundering into our ears day in and day out and from countless persons and platforms. Shutting it out is the problem, for nonsense has subtle ways of creeping upon us. True, we must know something of such inanities in order to strengthen our immunity to them; but a few minutes of listening a week should enable us to recognize the fallacy of these noisy voices the moment one of them is heard.

The other Voice Without—the voice of wisdom—demands skilled listening, at all times, and with no prejudices as to source. Have in mind that "immense hidden powers lurk in the unconscious of the most common man—indeed, of all people without exception."[2] It behooves each of us to be constantly on the lookout for this hidden power from unexpected sources.

Skilled receptivity requires that we "unscreen" or unmask ourselves.

When you are in a receptive state of mind, things can be easily understood; you are listening when your real attention is given to something. But unfortunately most of us

---
[2]*Ibid.,* p. 53.

listen through a screen of resistances. We are screened
with prejudices, whether religious or spiritual, psychological or scientific; or with daily worries, desires and fears.
And with these as a screen we listen. Therefore, we listen
really to our own noises, to our own sound, not to what is
being said.[3]

"What is being said," in its most profound sense, in-
cludes not only all the truth and righteousness currently in
expression but everything that has been said during recorded
history. There is more or less of the seer in all who now live or
ever have inhabited this earth. Listen!

THE VOICE WITHIN

As distinguished from the process of hearing the Voices
Without, listening to the Voice Within is shrouded in mystery.
This Voice has been variously described as creativity, insight,
intuition, invention, discovery, flashes of enlightenment—
ideas coming to mind from who knows where! All the truth
and righteousness known to man originates as the Voice
Within. It is here, in ourselves as well as in others, that immense hidden powers lurk in the unconscious depths, that
potentialities await tapping.

As Hamlet says:

> There are more things in Heaven and earth, Horatio,
>   Then are dreamt of in your philosophy.

I doubt that there is any proven or perfect formula for ef-

---

[3]J. Kirshnamurti, *The First and Last Personal Freedom.*

fective listening to the Voice Within. No two persons' preparations are or ever have been the same, no hearings ever identical. Variations in hearers and in what's heard! Why? This is a tuning-in problem and each receiving set is different. Your amplifier may be far more powerful than mine, and you may be able to tune in frequencies undreamed of by me. The best instruction is always nebulous, never precise. Example:

> My instinct tells me that everything hinges on resiliency, courage and stamina with which we succeed in seeing beyond the darkness [listening over and beyond the silence], penetrating the noxious, transcending dismay, corruption, asserting grace. By grace I mean vision, illumination, absorption in the beneficent totality to which we belong.

While I regard this as a splendid observation by Richard Guggenheimer and beautifully phrased, reflect on how uninstructive it is for one who aspires to listen, but never has attuned himself to the Voice Within. All such observations are nebulous, and indeed must be so for this is an esoteric phenomenon shrouded in mystery.

THE UNDISCOVERED SELF

As to my own experiences, listening to the Voices Without has been self-directed; no "educators" have told me to whom I should listen. I have gone where my inquisitive nose has led me, harkening to those voices which enlighten along the lines of my own unique interests and aspirations. I am by no means a certified scholar.

Where lies the truth that can make us free? In the undiscovered self—listening to the Voice Within! As to this phase of listening, my experiences, relative to some others I know about, are trivial. Yet, I have heard enough to free myself of know-it-all-ness. An infinite unknown has made itself apparent; I stand in awe of everything from atoms to galaxies, from a blade of grass to the human cortex. Further, I am aware of "immense *hidden* powers" lurking within me and I know that listening to the Voice Within is the only key, the single way, of freeing these powers from their unconscious depths.

What is this art? As already suggested, what works for one may be a futile technique for any other. Yet, as I shall try to demonstrate in another chapter, there is a benefit to those who receive, if not to others, in sharing what they have learned from listening to the Voice Within.

Here is my formula for whatever it is worth: Get all daily chores into the past tense. Free the self from fretting, worries, stresses, anxieties in order to be in a joyous frame of mind. Take a problem to which an answer is desired but not apparent. Concentrate, that is, prepare to think it through. An idea will come to mind, sometimes in minutes.[4] Write it down. Then, if one is on the right wave length, explanatory ideas will flow, often in rapid succession. And there, finally, is the problem clarified as if by magic.[5] How does one explain this

---

[4]Not always in minutes; I tried time after time over a span of twenty years to explain why the Biblical injunction, "Resist not evil," is a wise guideline. Stick-to-it-ness finally resulted in an explanation satisfactory to me. See my *Then Truth Will Out,* Irvington, N.Y., 1971, pp. 118-124.

[5]Speaking of magic, the several quotes in this chapter appeared to me for the first time after I began its writing, a phenomenon I have experienced for years. Relevant ideas put in an appearance when one is ready for them. What law is at work here? The Law of Readiness, perhaps?

flow? If anyone really knows, I do not know who he is. The mood in which my formula is rooted has to be prayerful—desired above all else.

A JOYOUS FRAME OF MIND

Why is it necessary to be in a joyous frame of mind? Perhaps there is no earthly experience that is attended by greater exuberance than hearing the Voice Within, than unmasking one's unconscious depths. If listening is to have this result it must be undertaken or anticipated in a similar frame of mind. No happy ending ever stemmed from a distraught or angry start. "Everything hinges on resiliency," and that is what joyousness assures.

One more important point. Unmasking the unconscious depths is not a now-and-then game. If it cannot be made a continuing way of life, forget it. True, whenever listening to the Voice Within results in an enlightenment, one wonders what comes next. And the secret is to keep wondering, listening but never pushing. Over-anxiety is a foe. Relax and have faith; the next step will show itself. Take that step at once; get it into the past tense, making way for yet another. This stairway has no ending.

Who's Listening? is listed as my seventeenth book. But like most of the others, it is not really a book. The following chapters are but recordings of what I have learned from listening during recent months—and put between two covers. But each chapter does have a bearing on a deep and abiding interest shared by thousands: human freedom. Repetition here and there I acknowledge, but my excuse is that "Repetition is the mother of learning."

I hereby share these recordings with whoever cares to listen. Who will listen to the responses, be they critical or approving? I will!

2

THOU FOOL

*No wind makes for him who has
no destined port.*

—MONTAIGNE

Readiness is all! For some years I have thought of this as a truth, but only in the past few months have repeated experiences caused me to refer, in my own mind, to "the Law of Readiness," so profound does this truth now seem to me. In a word, there is a uniformity at work here, as absolute as the Law of Gravitation.

The most recent experience: Beginning only a few days ago I had a nagging urge to explain how stupid it is to call anyone stupid, or even think that of others! Name calling is a temptation whenever someone does not see what I see or when he acts in ways I do not approve. No ideas flashed into mind as to how this subject should be approached. However, the subject was simmering in my subconscious: I was "ready." Then the following experiences in rapid succession:

11

1. This sentence by a famous German psychiatrist, Dr. Fritz Kunkel:

> But we have only one book which gives us the full description of the human situation, and of the way leading through all troubles and frustrations, and finally into utmost light. It is the great textbook of depth-psychology: The New Testament.[1]

2. Next, a letter from Spokane and this quotation by another psychiatrist, Dr. James T. Fisher:

> If you were to take the sum total of all the authoritative articles ever written by the most qualified of psychologists and psychiatrists on the subject of mental hygiene—if you were to combine and refine them and cleave out the excess verbiage—if you were to take the whole of the meat and none of the parsley, and if you were to have these unadulterated bits of pure scientific knowledge concisely expressed by the most capable of living poets, you would have an awkward and incomplete summation of the Sermon on the Mount.

3. The Sermon on the Mount! How well did I know this? Much too casually! An evening or two later there appeared on my bedside reading table, as if by magic, *The Concise Bible,* a condensed rendition of the King James version, a book I had not opened since its publication eleven years ago.[2] I reread the Sermon on the Mount for the first time in many years. And there was my article:

---

[1] Kunkel, *op. cit.,* p. 28.
[2] Frances Hazlitt, *The Concise Bible,* Chicago, 1962, p. 126.

. . . whosoever shall say, Thou fool, shall be in danger of hell fire.

Just what is meant by "hell fire"? While not certain, I take it to be a theological expression suggesting destruction of the self—as contrasted with intellectual and spiritual unfoldment: growth in consciousness. At least, such an interpretation is in line with my thesis.

The New Testament in Modern English puts it this way: "and anyone who looks down on his brother as a *lost soul* is himself heading straight for the fire of destruction."

The New English Bible: ". . . if he *sneers* at him [his brother] he will have to answer it in the fires of hell."

I prefer "Thou fool" to "lost soul" or "sneer" simply because calling another "a fool" comes closer to that contemptuous attitude I find difficult to overcome, namely, "He's stupid."

THE LAW OF READINESS

Good background for this thesis is furnished by the Law of Readiness. Many people, when the matter is broached, refuse to acknowledge any such law. Why? Probably because they have had no experiences that suggest such a law and, further, they will claim that this law cannot be verified statistically. Indeed, it cannot! Here, however, is my point: Only an infinitesimal number of the laws that govern the Cosmic Order are known to man; most are forever beyond his perception. Verification, therefore, in the vast majority of instances, is beyond the reach of science so-called. No person perceives more than a glimpse of Infinite Truth and no two perceptions are ever identical. If those who do not see eye to eye with me are fools, then what am I, who do not see eye to eye with them!

For instance, I observe people who simultaneously applaud the moon ventures and complain bitterly about rising prices. I clearly see the correlation; they see no relationship whatsoever between enormous government expenditures and the high cost of living. Am I to call them stupid simply because they are not ready to grasp the connection?

A MISSED CONNECTION

At a meeting of housing contractors, the members were exultant over the two million new starts predicted for the year ahead. But they fail to realize that most of these are military or public housing starts or projects otherwise financed by government. Further, they detect no relationship between government subsidies and the unbelievable specifications now dictated by government to cover the merest detail—such as the required thickness, down to a fraction of an inch, for the floor of a kitchen cabinet. "Who pays the fiddler calls the tune" is a truism they fail to grasp. Am I who sees this to sneer at them, to call them lost souls, to exclaim, "thou fools" because they are not ready for my explanations?

Put me in an audience and let Beethoven himself lecture on musical composition. What would be elementary for him would be incomprehensible to me. Is Beethoven warranted in calling me stupid? If so, I am a thousand and one fools for there is an infinity of subjects about which I am ignorant, and this also is your condition whoever you are. To call another a fool is to proclaim oneself a universal genius. "Perfection does not exist," said Alfred de Musset, "to expect to possess it is the most dangerous kind of madness."

True, I have improved my manners to the point where I no longer call anyone a fool to his face. Outwardly, I have overcome this frightful trait; inwardly, not quite! This is to infer that I have hopes of erasing it from my thinking.

Calling Joe Doakes a fool or stupid harms him little if at all. The damage is to me in that I gain his enmity. He will no longer hear me, whatever wisdom I have to offer. This is to sink one's own ship. But this is not the half of it!

A COURSE OF SELF-DESTRUCTION

The key to my main point is found in the translation which reads, ". . . and anyone who *looks down* on his brother as a lost soul is himself heading straight for the fire of destruction." In a word, the contemptuous subordination of another person—the entertainment of such a thought, even when silent—spells self-destruction. Rid ourselves of this inner fault or "face the danger of hell fire."

Those who offer us this advice assume, of course, that it is addressed to that man who has a "destined port," as Montaigne phrases it. Unless a person is aiming for growth in consciousness—becoming what he is not yet—then the point has no more relevance to the human being than to any nonentity. Actually, I am trying to think a way out of this fault mostly for myself or for anyone interested "in going places."

Reflect on our kindly attitude toward humbler forms of life, an oyster, say, or a bumblebee. It never enters our heads to think of them as stupid or foolish. Why? They are so low on the scale of consciousness that the categories do not apply. But the higher the consciousness the more are we inclined to use derogatory terms; people occasionally refer to their horses, dogs, and cats as stupid. And when it comes to human beings, this tendency reaches its apogee. *The higher the consciousness the higher pitched is the derision!* I insist that this is irrational.

If entirely rational, we would no more refer to a fellow being than a bumblebee as stupid. *This does not signify approval of everyone else;* it has only to do with avoiding self-destruction.

A PLEA FOR TOLERANCE

Speaking of Readiness, at this very point, while drafting this chapter, I received a letter enclosing a prayer containing, among others, these four petitions:

- Release me from the craving habit to straighten out everybody's affairs.
- Make me thoughtful but not moody; helpful but not bossy.
- Teach me the glorious lesson that I may be mistaken.
- I dare not ask for improved memory, but for a growing humility and less cocksureness. . . .

That man, by the act of framing his own rational petitions, is freeing himself from irrationality. He is not trying to run the world or to occupy the final judgment seat. He is free to grow in consciousness simply because he has consciously rid himself of such obsessive preoccupations as referring to others as stupid or "Thou fool."

Growth in consciousness is possible only in intellectual and spiritual freedom, that is, when the self is freed from managing or judging the lives of others.

The better world begins with that man who attends to his inner freedom. Would you have your counsel more widely sought? Emulate that man. To find the way, ask yourself this question: With whom would I rather dine tonight, that man or an angry, know-it-all person? That man is my answer and doubtless is yours.

3

ECONOMIC READINESS

. . . a light we term self-interest,
which is so illuminating, so con-
stant, and so penetrating, when it
is left free of hindrance.

—BASTIAT

While writing the introductory chapter of this book, I was thinking my way through this matter of "readiness." I suspected a Law of Readiness, but not until I had worked on the second chapter did the suspicion become a certainty.

My readiness to believe there is such a thing as a universal Law of Readiness will lead some of my friends to chide me for my impracticality and mysticism, as occasionally they have done. I am now ready to explain why this is one of the most practical ideas I have ever come upon, an idea that has been governing our lives for centuries though we may not have known it. This Law is fundamental to sound economics and we ignore or disobey it to our peril.

How did I arrive at this discovery? Not by myself, but by listening! An associate of mine, after reading the preceding chapter, remarked, "It seems to me that your Law of Readiness relates just as much to the business of our daily affairs as to the flow of philosophical ideas." He suggested that Frederic Bastiat's explanation of the provisioning of Paris, written well over a century ago, was a perfect illustration of this point. And it is!

On coming to Paris for a visit, I said to myself: Here are a million human beings who would all die in a few days if supplies of all sorts did not flow into this great metropolis. It staggers the imagination to try to comprehend the vast multiplicity of objects that must pass through its gates tomorrow, if its inhabitants are to be preserved from the horrors of famine, insurrection, and pillage. And yet all are sleeping peacefully at this moment, without being disturbed for a single instant by the idea of so frightful a prospect. On the other hand, eighty departments [provinces] have worked today, without co-operative planning or mutual arrangements, to keep Paris supplied. How does each succeeding day manage to bring to this gigantic market just what is necessary—neither too much nor too little? What, then, is the resourceful and secret power that governs the amazing regularity of such complicated movements, a regularity in which everyone has such implicit faith, although his prosperity and his very life depend upon it? That power is an *absolute principle, the principle of free exchange.*

MOTIVATED BY SELF-INTEREST

Now, what is it that motivates, activates, "illuminates" this principle? Harken to Bastiat's next sentence:

We put our faith in that inner light which Providence has placed in the hearts of all men, and to which has been entrusted the preservation and the unlimited improvement of our species, a light we term self-interest, which is so illuminating, so constant, and so penetrating, when it is left free of hindrance.

A FRIGHTFUL ALTERNATIVE

What is this absolute principle's nemesis, the hindrance to be guarded against if disaster is to be avoided? Bastiat gave us the answer:

Where would you be, inhabitants of Paris, if some cabinet minister decided to substitute for that power contrivances of his own invention, however superior we might suppose them to be; if he proposed to subject this prodigious mechanism to his supreme direction, to take control of all of it into his own hands, to determine by whom, where, how, and under what conditions everything should be produced, transported, exchanged, and consumed? Although there may be much suffering within your walls, although misery, despair, and perhaps starvation, cause more tears to flow than your warm-hearted charity can wipe away, it is probable, I dare say certain, that the arbitrary intervention of the government would infinitely multiply this suffering and spread among all of you the ills that now affect only a small number of your fellow citizens.[1]

Let's try to understand the part played here by the Law of Readiness as it applies to the generation of both intellectual

---

[1]Frederic Bastiat, *Economic Sophisms,* Irvington, N.Y., 1968, pp. 97-98.

and material goods. When I aspire to possess ideas not yet known to me, and prepare by freeing myself from inner conflicts—resistance due to fear, anger, anxiety, know-it-all-ness, and the like—in a word, when I am in a state of readiness, the ideas mysteriously enter my mind—admittedly, only a fraction of what would be mine were I better prepared! Similarly, liberty in society and freedom in transactions prepares the situation in which material goods mysteriously appear.

A MATTER OF IMPLICIT FAITH

There is no distinction in principle between ideas flowing into my mind and goods flowing into the hands of Parisians. The inhabitants of Paris needed the goods as you and I need ideas. And they were in a state of readiness for them; there was a market demand. Bastiat refers to "this secret power," another way of acknowledging the mysteriousness of this Law. Note, also, that the people had an "implicit faith" that the goods would be on hand to accommodate their readiness, precisely as I have an implicit faith that your phone will ring when I dial your number. This faith extends to countless goods and services. Mysterious? There is not a person on this earth who knows what makes that phone ring. Name one who can define electricity!

Suppose no one had ever invented an alphabet. Language would be at the level of grunts and groans. No earthly person would have readied himself for a pencil. As it is, we readied ourselves for pencils. Do they appear? Yes, and mysteriously! Why do I say this? No person knows how to make a pen or pencil, yet billions of these writing tools are made annually.[2]

Or, suppose no one had ever originated the concept of zero. There would be no dishwashers, autos, jet planes. Astronomy would be limited to the range of the naked eye—no telescopes. The accomplishments of modern chemistry and physics would be out of the question with Roman numerals.

Reflect on these things which so mysteriously appear. What are they, really? What is "this secret power," as Bastiat phrases it? This is clearly a spiritual phenomenon in the sense that insight, intuition, invention, discovery, creativity, the spirit of inquiry are spiritual. Everything by which we live, be it a can opener or a windowpane, requires spiritual development before it manifests itself in the material. In a word, *ideas*! Ideas, be they entirely philosophical or of the kind that feed and clothe us, respond only to the Law of Readiness.

ENTER THE MEDDLER

Bastiat saw more clearly through the political fog than any other thinker and writer known to me. He accurately pinpointed the nemesis to the principle of free exchange and free market pricing by his reference to a "cabinet officer" who thinks he can substitute his own know-it-all-ness for this mysterious "prodigious mechanism." The bureaucrat, whoever he is, no more knows what causes the phone to ring or how a pencil or windowpane is made than I do. *He is*

[2]See my *Anything That's Peaceful,* Irvington, N.Y., 1964, pp. 136-143.

distinguished by not knowing how little he knows. The extent to which we entrust our lives to these arbitrary interventions by government, to that extent will we multiply our suffering and spread among all of us the ills that now affect only a small number of our fellowmen. Once we become aware of the Law of Readiness, the reason becomes crystal clear, for the Law is exemplified whenever economic transactions freely occur.

A point to remember: We can only become aware of this Law; we shall never understand it. Analogously, we do not understand electricity but we are aware of its powers and harness them to our use. We do not understand gravitation, yet we know enough of its nature to count on skiing downhill rather than uphill, parachuting to the earth rather than into space. We can gain, at best, an awareness of hidden or secret powers and how to employ them. But we are not helped to understand such mysteries by becoming a "cabinet officer." This is one fact we can understand!

Readiness is a phenomenon that requires freedom, and freedom is of two sorts: outer and inner. The nemeses of freedom are resistances. As I have already suggested, the nemeses to inner freedom are fear, anger, stress, know-it-allness, and the like. Rid ourselves of these or the Law of Readiness is inoperative. Ideas cannot flow into a consciousness that is thus barricaded.

COERCIVE INTERVENTION

The nemeses to outer freedom are also resistances. They are coercive impositions by other persons. Other people are to run our lives and not we ourselves! A mere sampling of regimented actions: the hours of labor, the wages paid, what and with whom we may exchange and the prices permitted, even the thoughts we shall entertain (government dictated school curricula, for instance). How, in heaven's name, can I ready myself for the flow of goods and services when I am not allowed to enter the stream of economic activities except as a caricature of what bureaucrats think I should resemble! And with every single one of them having a different view of what that caricature should be! Carry this way of life to its logical conclusion and I am no longer a man but only putty to be molded—and by whom?

WHO IS MORE COMPETENT?

My answer: By persons afflicted with "the most dangerous kind of madness": those so blind to their own imperfections that they naively believe they can manage your life better than you can. Choose any dictocrat who has ever lived and ask yourself, is he or you the more competent to guide your life? The answer in every instance comes loud and clear. It's you by a mile! Dictocrats are victims of conceit and, by reason of their conceit, have failed to ready themselves. Therefore, they are utterly incapable of contributing to the readying process for their fellow men. Each of them is the nemesis of readiness. Further, this domineering trait will continue to grow and spread until we come to recognize its fatal nature and abandon it—voluntarily.

As to the Law of Readiness, let me confess here that I understate my indebtedness when I say that I have been readied a trillion times more by others than I have readied myself or contributed to the readiness of any person.

THE ENTREPRENEUR

Finally, in this matter of economic readiness, let us consider the spirit of entrepreneurship. And I mean far more by this than the dictionary definition: "a person who organizes and manages a business undertaking, assuming the risk for the sake of the profit." Conceded, organizing ability and the hope for profit may be included in the constitution of entrepreneurs. But many people have both organizing ability and a craving for profit, yet they are utter failures. What is the gift that distinguishes the successful entrepreneur? It is a rare readiness, a foresight, that is, an ability to anticipate what people will want.

Are people ready for pencils, computers, or whatever? Not a one of these items would be available in the absence of individuals who could read the readiness of customers in its dormant stage and then organize the varied talents—individuals in unique states of readiness—to serve that potential demand. All the readiness among human beings for this or that would lie dormant and unserved were it not for the spirit of entrepreneurship. Interestingly enough and quite mysteriously, entrepreneurs appear on the scene to accommodate readiness. That is, they appear *if* they are free to act!

Under what conditions then does the Law of Readiness best work its wonders? Freedom! Inner and outer freedom! Freedom from personal frustrations and freedom from coercive restraints against creative action! Why not try freedom and, by so doing, harness the secrets of the Universe to the evolution of mankind!

4

YOU RASCAL, YOU!

From whence come wars and fight-
ing among you? come they not
hence, even of your lusts that war
in your number?

—JAMES 4: 1

As with all of my "original" ideas, this one turns out to be
"old hat." Upon reading the first draft, an associate remarked, "Why, that is precisely what the Bible says." Thus,
the above quote. There then came to mind an essay we published several years ago entitled "Big Wars from Little Errors Grow."[1] Old hat or not, the theme needs constant repetition; it is so easily forgotten.

As I view the societal scene from my modest place in it,
four current phenomena are outstandingly impressive:

1. Things on the surface, at least, appear to be amiss, not
   only in the U.S.A. but world-wide: wars with guns,
   wars with words in religion, education, business, politics, brutishness on the campuses as on the streets.

---

[1] E. W. Dykes in *The Freeman,* January 1964.

Never in my lifetime have the confrontations been more pronounced.

2. An amazing awakening to the fact that things are amiss: countless admissions by persons on all sides of the politico-economic argument—scholarly intellectuals, columnists, politicians, and others—many of whom have had a hand in bringing on the very calamity they now decry.

3. A frenzied search for explanations, causes, reasons— of the most diverse nature. These range from an incompetent bureaucracy to tax loopholes to inequality of income to excessive or inadequate welfarism to economic growth to lagging GNP—you name it! Never have the assigned reasons been more at odds and, as I see it, more astray.

4. A widespread acknowledgment of trouble but without any noticeable confession of personal shortcomings. Nearly every finger points at someone else; it is impressively *you*; there is hardly an *I* in the population.

Imagine! All of this rascality and not a professed rascal among us! Why? It is simply because the real evil, the cause of our waywardness, is rarely suspected. Thus, self-identification is impossible. People do not link themselves to error about which they are unaware.

THE DOMINEERING HABIT

What is this rascality? It is the domineering habit, the insistence that others act in accord with one's own shadowy lights. Perhaps no one has shaken this habit completely, so common is its practice. This habit has its inception in the closest relationships, as in the family, one parent lording it over the other or both of them assuming an authoritarian as distinguished from an exemplary relationship with their children. It takes such seemingly innocent forms as do-as-I-say—a carbon copy way of life.

This tendency, once rooted, spreads by unseen degrees to neighbors, the classroom, the pulpit, and other associations. Sooner or later, it begins to grow teeth and takes the form of do-as-I-say-*or-else,* that is, it explodes into out-and-out coercion as in countless thousands of unprincipled governmental compulsions. When not recognized as evil and thus unchecked, it brings on dictatorships and finally reaches its apogee, its most vicious manifestation: mass slaughter.

MAN LORDING OVER MAN

I am unaware of any evil more pronounced than man lording it over man. Not even God does this. Indeed, He has given us a freedom so radical that we may deny our Maker or otherwise make fools of ourselves. As I see it, the domineering habit is the root of all evil[2] and unless there is some realization that it is, we will continue to ascribe nonreasons for our troubles and without anyone faulting himself. We will go on exclaiming, "You rascal, you!"

Enough of my theorizing. Let us reflect on an observed

---

[2]This is close to the idea of Original Sin, as many theologians define it: the tendency of the creature to try to usurp the role of the Creator. That interpretation appears to be in accord with the Biblical account which describes the tempter as telling the human creature that if he will eat the forbidden fruit he can become like God. Genesis 3:5. See also William Temple, *Nature, Man and God,* London, 1934, p. 496 ff.

fact: an example cannot be found where domineering in practice—man lording it over man—has resulted in success.[3] The record is failure, without exception. It has to be. A carbon copy is never as good as the imperfect original.

Markedly on the increase are the complaints I hear from fathers and mothers about the waywardness of their children. In some instances, drugs. But most of them go like this: "She is brilliant, a straight A student in college, but she has bought the whole socialistic doctrine. She won't do as I say. How do I solve this problem?" I have yet to hear one of these do-as-I-say parents confess, "The fault is mine." In far too many of these relationships an unsuspected domineering attitude has been substituted for parental cooperation and guidance.

TWO CASES OF DOMINEERING:
SCHOOLING AND POSTAL SERVICE

Take two cases of domineering that have "teeth": government education and the government postal service.

Government education has three forms of domineering: compulsory attendance, government dictation of the curricula, and the forcible collection of the wherewithal to pay the bills. That education in America is in a mess goes without saying. It is generally conceded, even by many educators. Show me one person who says, "The fault is mine." *Yet,*

---

[3]Success is composed of gains, not losses. Sputniks, moon ventures, the Gateway Arch, and the like—ambitions of a few—are made possible by enormous losses on the part of millions of people. With justice or fairness as the premise, these are failures.

*it is the fault of everyone who has had any part in endorsing
or supporting or practicing any form of domineering!*[4]

The government postal service never, even remotely,
matched what a free market operation would have accomplished. And it is getting worse day by day. Can you name
one person during the past century who confessed the fault
is his? No one makes such an admission because he does
not recognize the domineering trait as the root of the failure.

The railroads have been subjected to domineering with
"teeth" for decades. They are failing. Not a person takes
the blame; it is now and always has been, "You rascal, you!"
There is no end to the illustrations that could be given.

As already stated, the domineering habit has its inception
in the closest relationships. Correct it here and it will cease
to be a menace elsewhere. Let us return, for illustration,
to those parents whose children refuse to share parental
views, conform to parental dictates.

PARTNERS IN LEARNING

True, these parents are unaware that they have been domineering and such recognition is indeed difficult. As parents,
we tend to forget the growth we ourselves experienced during childhood and adolescence. By the time we reach parenthood, our own growth may have stopped. We have arrived,
that is, we no longer feel that need to learn which we

---

[4]This is not "collective guilt" as some would have it but individual error
piled high. And, critics to the contrary, each of us is to some extent
shaped by the environment in which we find ourselves. In another kind of
world, you and I would be in another kind of endeavor.

want our children to feel. If they would only do as we say—think as we do—that would be good enough! The insistence that our children do what we ourselves refuse to do is what destroys the proper relationships; there is no longer a learning partnership. Our failure to maintain this kinship in learning is a form of domineering. Looked at from the child's point of view, he is a know-nothing and the parent the know-it-all. Conflict!

Perhaps the best way to shed light on the proper relationship between you and me, husband and wife, parent and child—all close relationships—is to cite an actual case between a teacher and one of his students. My introduction began with a letter from the student, a stranger to me. Here it is, abbreviated:

> Sir, I am a freshman at a college in Florida. Seven short months ago I came here believing in Keynesian economics. That is what I had been taught in high school and I had accepted it without question. Since coming here I have been made aware of these fallacies, and due to my teacher, ————. It is like I have been blind and suddenly recovered my sight.

A few days later, the teacher, also a stranger to me and unaware of the student's letter, wrote in part:

> I am a Social Science professor at a private, small liberal arts college. I am very much interested in the freedom point of view and, for the last few months, *have spent time trying to understand the view.* (Italics added)

Fascinated with these two letters, I invited the professor to one of our Seminars. In getting to know him, I discovered what turned the student from socialism to a free market point of view. This professor is trying to understand; he and his students are partners in the learning process. *They have a common goal: enlightenment!* Contrast this with the parent whose goal is to make the child a carbon copy of himself. The parent may not think of this as domineering, but he gives that impression to the youngster. In this circumstance, the parent and child are not in partnership but in conflict. This matter of posture applies in all close relationships.

If we wish to put an end to the more horrible consequences of the domineering habit such as state socialism and eventually mass murder, we can do so by nipping it in the bud. This is to say, rid ourselves of the habit where it is born, namely, in our close relationships, whatever they happen to be.

Riddance requires no more than (1) an awareness that the domineering habit—freedom's opposite—is the root of all evil, (2) an ability to recognize domineering in ourselves and to be done with it, (3) an appreciation that learning is just as much a requirement for the parent as the child, for the teacher as the student, for me as you, as much needed at eighty as eight and, (4) a strict observance of the Golden Rule.

Once we recognize that the vicious domineering of dictators is but the political extremity of the domineering habit that lurks in the mill run of us, we should exclaim, "You rascal, you!" only to the image we see in the mirror. Breaking ourselves of a bad habit is the way to destroy its most malicious manifestation. Remove the source—that's all.

5

PILOT ERRORS

*Error of opinion may be tolerated
where reason is left free to combat
it.*

—JEFFERSON

It was year's end, December 31, 1972. One of my journal entries for the day:

> The *New York Sunday Times* reports as a disaster the crash of a jumbo jet in the Florida Everglades. And on the same page a mere announcement that "the President is willing to name union men to all Federal departments." In my judgment, the latter is by far the greater disaster in the long run. The jet crash, I suspect, was due to pilot error; naming union men to all Federal departments, I am certain, is also pilot error.

I have no respect for organizations as such—be they labor unions, chambers of commerce, organized religions, educational organizations, governments, or whatever. Respect can be extended only to individual persons who uphold and practice the several virtues. A person's membership in this organization or that may reveal much or nothing.

An organization is analogous to a book defined as an assemblage of pages bound between two covers. Books, as such, do not merit respect; it is the content that counts. Books range all the way from filth and pornography to intellectual and spiritual enlightenment as found in the Bible or in *The Wealth of Nations*. The vices and virtues between the covers of organizations are no less diverse. The content of each must be examined.

WHY UNION REPRESENTATION?

Why do we not witness the political pilot's willingness to name chamber of commerce men to all Federal departments? Or members of the Women's Liberation movement? Or Catholics, Lutherans, Episcopalians, Holy Rollers? Or corporate executives? Or Farm Bureau members? Or certified accountants? Or physicians? Why single out union members? From the standpoint of good government, there is no more logic in naming the latter than the others. There is, of course, a "reason."

And the "reason" is not that union members are distinguished beyond all others in the population for their statesmanship; they do not exhibit devotion to a common, across-the-board justice, free market and private ownership understanding and practice, or a disdain of special privilege! The real reason? Labor unions, more than any other labeled segment of the population, dictate what governments—Federal, state and local—shall and shall not do. Naming union men to all Federal departments is but an acknowledgment of their overpowering influence. It is a resignation to a political fact and I believe that this resignation, in itself, is a disaster. Find, if you will, any other reason for this "if you can't lick 'em, jine 'em" attitude!

Before assaying the disastrous effects of resignation, let us reflect on the policies we are giving in to, admitting help-lessness before, accepting as *fait accompli.*

THE QUEST FOR POLITICAL POWER

Union men, by and large—or their officials, at least—sincerely believe in gaining political power, in "running the show." They regard this as a proper aspiration and, in this respect, are not to be distinguished from most of their opponents—the losers—the ones who also seek political power but with their men in the driver's seat rather than unionists. Virtually all contestants in the political arena are striving to get themselves in a position from which they can run the show. There is little attention to the philosophical issue: domineering versus freedom; the contest is which side shall have the dictatorial say-so. Most people who criticize union men should hark to Cicero's advice: "Everything you reprove in another, you must carefully avoid in yourself."

Very well! Having agreed that union men differ little from the mill run of humanity over the ages, let us now have a look at the policies they espouse.

A cartel is defined as "an association of industrialists for establishing a monopoly by price fixing, etc." Labor unions are no less cartels than are some industrial combines. They are price fixers; this is their chief claim to fame. They fix prices not by voluntary agreement but by edict backed by violence. Monopolists? Try to become a 747 Captain for less than $57,000 a year or a plumber in Westchester County for less than $15.80 an hour plus the contractor's percentage.

All above-market wage rates forcibly exacted by labor unions cause unemployment precisely as $20 for a pound of cheese would cause its unemployment at the table. How is this unemployment catastrophe covered up? Labor unions, using their political power, get the government to pick up the tab: public housing, urban renewal, the Gateway Arch, moon shots, and thousands of other pyramids—"make work" projects to employ resources which have been coercively excluded from the market.[1]

These "make work" projects cost billions upon billions annually. How does government pay these enormous bills? First, by direct taxation—all the voters will tolerate. This, however, is far from adequate. How make up the difference? Increase the money supply: *inflation!* The result? The dollar becomes worth less and less. It has lost nearly 70 per cent of its purchasing value in the past 33 years. As one perceptive wit phrases it: "Nothing can replace the American dollar—and it practically has."

THE "NEW ECONOMICS"

Reflect on this problem realistically. If it were generally believed that these tactics of labor unions were leading us

---

[1]The so-called Full Employment Act of 1946 authorizes governmental spending and relief programs to employ over-priced labor and other resources for purposes for which there are no willing customers. For further discussion see Henry Hazlitt, *The Failure of the "New Economics,"* Princeton, N.J., 1959, pp. 399-408.

to disaster, citizens would have none of them. Indeed, union men themselves would not be a party to what they now applaud.

But the general belief is to the contrary. Tactics such as these comprise "the new economics" and they are given prestige by such celebrated characters as Lord John Maynard Keynes, as well as by thousands of so-called economists spawned by them. These tactics are now believed to lead not to disaster but to prosperity and social welfare. Old fogeys may still frown on wage rates fixed above the market by violence, with government taxation and inflation to pick up the tab for the resulting unemployment; but why fret when assured that the consequence is all to the good! So goes the "reasoning."

As if "the new economics" were really new! Actually, all of this is an inheritance from our barbaric ancestors. It rests on the primitive notion that these self-appointed rulers are capable of running the lives of others beneficially. The fact? No person who has ever lived has such a capability over any single individual, let alone over millions. All wielders of this kind of power resemble the rest of us in knowing substantially nothing, but they are unaware of how little they know. All of "the new economics" is old hat.

NEW IDEAS ARE UNSTABLE

I am trying to suggest that *beliefs* are here at issue. And at stake is the overthrow of the newest and most enlightening thoughts in human history, that is, as pertaining to political economy: free, voluntary exchange, private ownership, and limited government concepts. Were we to collapse life on this earth into a calendar year, these ideas have been perceived during the last 3½ seconds before midnight of December 31. However, as Ortega points out, it is always the latest and highest acquisitions of the mind that are the least stable and the first to be abandoned whenever crisis threatens. The new, the wonderful—individual freedom—is now being abandoned in favor of the old, the primitive, the domineering way of life.

Sound economics is about as simple as this: Were the price of cheese to be coercively fixed at, say, $20 per pound, there would be no consumption. And were it coercively fixed at, say, 2¢ per pound, there would be no production. I say to all political rigging, "Cheese it!"

Even if the political pilot gives in to "the new economics" by expressing a willingness that union men be named to all Federal departments, and even if millions of others evidence such resignation, I must hold out for freedom though I may seem to stand alone. My faith tells me, however, that there are thousands of others—The Remnant—who are determined to do the same.

6

SHELTERING IDEOLOGIES

Damn the magistrates who play,
"protect me, I'll protect you."
—PETRONIUS

Some things never change, apparently: the nature of politicians, as distinguished from statesmen, for example. There is camaraderie in the trade; they take care of each other. "You play ball with me, and I'll play ball with you." No wonder the Roman magistrates winked at one another when they met! However, I do not damn the politicians who play the game that Petronius so rightly decried. My attitude is rather one of pity: they do not know any better!

Let us define our terms. What is meant by ideology? It is "the study of ideas, their nature and source . . . the doctrines, opinions, or way of thinking of an individual, class, etc."

And sheltering? As used here, it means protection from life's problems—seeking refuge from difficulties—not by building and strengthening one's own intellectual and physical assets but by using force or coercion to live off the resources of others. In politico-economic parlance these sheltering

ideologies range from protectionism and state interventionism to socialism, welfarism, the planned economy, Nazism,
fascism, Fabianism, communism.

Though sorry for politicians who play the barbaric game
of logrolling, my sorrow extends even more to those citizens
who elevate politicians to their domineering positions. Why
are these low-caliber men in office? Simply because too many
voters themselves are of this caliber—they do as well as they
know how to do. The dominators in office merely echo those
in the population who believe their interests are best served
by living at the expense of others. Barbarism in both cases;
like begetting like!

HALF ANIMAL

Why this harsh term, barbarism? The animal world, except
for man, is guided by instincts. Man has lost most, not all, of
his instincts. And few human beings have acquired man's
distinctive features: *the ability to think for self, personally to
will conduct, to make moral decisions.* Those who are neither
animal nor man—trapped between the two—exhibit barbaric
behavior: less than animals in instinctual guidance and short
of man in rationality.

How may be decide whether a person is trapped at the
barbaric level or has ascended to the human level? There are
many ways, but this simple test in economics should suffice:
does an individual believe that one man's gain is another's
loss?

Why is it that the Golden Rule is not universally accepted

and applied as the only solution to the social problem? The answer is simple. Mr. Lippmann put his finger on the heart of the matter in saying that *the fear* that "one man's or one country's gain is another man's or another country's loss is undoubtedly the greatest obstacle to human progress. It is the most primitive of all our social feelings and the most persistent and obstinate prejudice which we retain from our barbarian ancestors. It is upon this prejudice that civilization has foundered again and again. It is upon this prejudice that all schemes of conquest and exploitation are engendered. It is this prejudice which causes almost all men to think that the Golden Rule is a counsel of perfection which cannot be followed in the world of affairs."[1]

Each person's position on the ladder of civilization is determined by the sheltering ideologies he condones or sponsors. If he subscribes to exploitation in one or more of countless forms, he has not thought his way out of primitive prejudices. If, on the other hand, he has freed his thinking of these superstitions, he is at the human level.

EVERYONE GAINS IN FREE TRADE

Except in the case of gambling and thievery (illegal), or state exploitation (legal, but identical in an economic sense), every gain of mine is someone else's gain as well. I value your product or service more than the cash paid or I would not have made the exchange. You value the cash more than the product or service or you would have retained your wares. Whenever and wherever there are voluntary exchanges, each

---

[1]Newton Dillaway, *Consent,* Lee's Summit, Missouri, 1967, p. 74.

party gains in his own judgment—the sole basis of assessing value.[2] No sheltering ideology here! No hint of exploitation! Each doing for others that which he would have them do for him—the free market way.

Conceded, many people have ascended above the primitive level in other than the politico-economic realm which we are discussing here. But in this area, if we are to judge a man by his urge to plunder others, the number of "saved souls" is distressingly small. Further, this sad trait is not confined to any one occupational category. This propensity to live at the expense of others is as much in evidence among businessmen as labor union members, among professors of economics and clergymen as politicians.

Let us further identify those who subscribe to—support, condone, promote—the sheltering ideologies.

First, there are businessmen who seek varying forms of government protection against competition, domestic or foreign. Such people are not to be distinguished from labor union members who seek above-market wage rates for themselves by excluding other workers from certain jobs. Each practice is backed by government and thus exploits taxpayers and consumers. In this same category are those educators who demand tenure and go on strike to enforce their demands—all in the name of academic freedom!

Next are the promoters of such public works as The Gateway Arch, Urban Renewal, or moon shots. They may be likened to the monarchs of ancient Egypt. The pyramids were built with slave labor; today's public works are built by

---

[2]For an explanation of this point see *Value and Price* by Bohm-Bawerk, South Holland, Illinois, Libertarian Press, 1960.

the coercively extorted income representing a portion of your labor and mine. What's the difference!

CONTROLS EXPLOIT US

Those who support rent control and all other forms of wage and price controls are afflicted with a sheltering ideology. Controls seem to be a plausible way of dealing with rising costs, which in turn result from an increase in the money supply: inflation. Inflation is a device for syphoning private property into the coffers of government, and will be activated whenever the costs of government rise to the point where they cannot be met by direct tax levies—inflation to make up the difference. These excessive costs result because other sheltering ideologies are practiced; prices rise as they would were everyone to practice counterfeiting. Wage and price controls hide the truth; they deprive buyers and sellers of the facts as to the demand for and the supply of goods and services. Thus, exploitation, which most people favor, can go on its merry way—people blinding themselves to reality!

Those who favor paying farmers not to farm—farm supports —are at precisely the same sheltering level as the American bureaucrats of the thirties who killed baby pigs to raise the price of pork, or the Brazilians who burned part of their coffee to raise the price of the balance. Exploitation of both consumers and taxpayers!

Physicians and dentists who support medicare and a system of licensing in order to suppress free entry and competition will, by and large, claim opposition to cartels and monopolies in the business world; they simply want their own cartel. "Dares thus the devil rebuke our sin! Dare thus the kettle say the pot is black!"[3]

Take account of the millions who favor unemployment insurance—a device so sheltering that many employables prefer their handouts coercively taken from taxpayers to earning their own way.

THE SOCIAL SECURITY MONSTROSITY

Who, we must ask, is free from sheltering ideologies in one or more of their numerous forms? If the above examples fail to embrace most of the population, then note the multitudes who favor Social Security. Nearly all educational, religious, and charitable institutions—not compelled by law to join in this economic monstrosity—have rushed to the trough. Favored, indeed!

Monstrosity? Reflect on the facts. ". . . the Social Security tax is not only rising faster than any other Federal tax but is also increasingly unfair to lower income workers. . . . The maximum Social Security tax rose from $60 in 1949 to $811 in 1971 and will jump to $1,324 in 1974."[4]

Here, however, is the shocker: not a cent of the billions collected in Social Security taxes is put in a reserve fund to pay beneficiaries—only IOU's in the form of government bonds. These billions are spent, as any other tax money, to defray the current costs of government. From what, then, are beneficiaries paid? From more taxes imposed at time of pay-

---

[3]Henry Fielding.
[4]*New York Times,* November 19, 1972, p. 18.

ment, a tax on the beneficiaries as well as on other taxpayers. The enormous cost of this sheltering program is one of the major causes of inflation. If the money in circulation continues to escalate as in the past 33 years, it will total $1.5 trillion by the year 2000. What will the Social Security beneficiary then be able to buy with his dollar? Substantially nothing![5]

The proper function of government—organized force—is to codify the taboos against destructive actions and to enforce them. All creative activities, including the practice of charity, are appropriately left to men acting freely, voluntarily, cooperatively, competitively, privately. This is the freedom philosophy. As I see it, anyone who advocates, supports, or condones governmental intervention into any of the creative areas is a victim of one or more of the sheltering ideologies. And that covers all but a very few indeed!

WOULD YOU LET THEM STARVE?

I know the rebuttal; we hear it everywhere, by TV, radio, the press, nearly all associations—business, religious, educational, or whatever. Its substance? How else are we to care for the poor, the unfortunate, the unemployed, the aged? As a result, faith in free men to create a good society has all but disappeared.

The fact is that not a one of these alleged remedies is working. Nothing better illustrates the truth of this observation than one other of the sheltering ideologies: the minimum

---

[5]For more explanation, see "Social Security Re-examined" by Paul L. Poirot, *The Freeman,* November 1965.

wage law. This popular panacea harms the very people it is supposed to assist, those on the lower rungs of the economic ladder. Workers whose skills are not valued by others at $1.60 per hour, for instance, are relegated to permanent unemployment. Economists, the world over, regardless of their other persuasions, are nearly unanimous on this point, and a moment's thought should tell us why.[6]

I insist that every sheltering ideology, be it Social Security, unemployment insurance, medicare, farm supports, wage and price controls, modern pyramids, teacher tenure, cartels, or whatever, has precisely the same debilitating, destructive effect as the minimum wage law. All of these, without exception, harm the very people they are foolishly designed to help. At the root of these panaceas is nothing but an unwillingness to think, a failure to rise out of the primitive and up to the human level.

As to the sheltering ideologies, rare, indeed, is the person who favors none; rare, also, is he who favors but one.

What shall we infer from this? Sheltering has a near-unanimous approval. The individual who stands for even one special privilege endorses the principle of coercive exploitation; by his actions he declares that living off others is morally admissible.

The way to test the validity of this coercive exploitation is to assume its unanimous practice. It becomes obvious then that everyone would perish! Parasites die in the absence of a host.

One further observation: to the extent that the responsi-

---

[6]See my *Then Truth Will Out, op. cit.,* pp. 61-66.

bility for self is removed, whether voluntarily surrendered or coercively taken over by governmental action, to that extent is denied the very essence of one's being, and the individual perishes by unseen degrees.

Man's laudable purpose is not to vegetate, to retire, to seek an escape from life—to be secure as in a coma; it is, instead, to get ever deeper into life, to grow. And this can be accomplished only by an increasing use of one's faculties, solving problems, surmounting obstacles. For it is an observed fact that the art of becoming is composed of acts of overcoming.

Why not be done with sheltering ideologies? As Maxwell Anderson wrote in his preface to *Knickerbocker Holiday* in 1938: "The guaranteed life turns out to be not only not free— it's not safe."

7

WHAT DO YOU HAVE AGAINST THE POOR?

The best lightning-rod for your
own protection is your own spine.
—EMERSON

Whenever he hears someone demand a minimum wage law or any other impediment to freedom in transactions, my friend asks in all seriousness, "What do you have against the poor?" His point is well-taken. Unquestionably, many sponsors of welfare schemes—the long-run effect of which is to kill the goose that lays the golden eggs—are well-intentioned. Their hearts, if not their heads, are in the right place. The idea that they are doing offense to the very persons they wish to help is a shocker—hopefully, an eye-opener.

Perhaps the first shock would stem from the thought that a minimum wage law might do injury to anyone at all. Possibly to the wealthy employer, but surely not to the poor! The fact, however, is that those who have little to offer in the way of marketable skills are marginal producers at best; their services are wanted by others only at very low wages. Indeed, the total disappearance of such marginal producers would scarcely affect the over-all economy. So my friend is quite right. It is primarily, if not entirely, the poor who stand to lose if wage rates are pegged artificially high; those who sponsor minimum wage laws behave as if they hold a grudge against the poor.

The fact that a fair share of these sponsors act from motives of sympathy or pity—that they bear no grudge—in no way changes the consequences of their actions. Nonetheless, they victimize the poor. They hurt most the ones they love—and all because they fail to recognize these simple facts:

1. The eternal problem of economics is to overcome scarcity.
2. Plenitude is achieved by the application of human energies to natural resources and to the exchange of the numerous specializations.
3. The value of anything to anyone is always a subjective judgment—whatever one is willing to give up or trade for something else.
4. Freedom of production and trade—the free market—is the goose that lays the golden eggs and all impediments to this process, to the extent of their force and coverage, are destructive—obstacles to plenitude.
5. Minimum wage laws of say $1.60 leave unemployed all persons whose services are not of that much value to others.
6. To the extent of the productive potential thus unemployed, to that extent is the number of golden eggs reduced. But far worse: to that extent is everyone who cannot produce up to $1.60 an hour decreed *waste* and relegated to the economic scrapheap.

Nearly all who think of themselves as professional economists, regardless of their differences on some matters, agree
that minimum wage laws inflict injury first and foremost
on the poor. Even the avowed socialist, Gunnar Myrdal, the
celebrated Swedish economist, turns thumbs down on this
economic monstrosity.[1] The writings of economists in support
of this point are plentiful, indeed.

SEEKERS OF PRIVILEGE

However, not all sponsors of minimum wage laws are
"good guys" lacking in economic sense. There are countless
thousands, perhaps a majority, whose motivations are mer-
cenary. The first type is to be found in labor union "leadership." The motivation here is to keep these low-wage,
marginal producers off the labor market, that is, to eliminate
them from competition. Permit no one to wait on table for,
say, $1.00 an hour, even if he wishes to do so, and the union
gains a monopoly of waiters' jobs. Call this crass materialism
or what you will, it is not inspired by sympathy or pity.

The second type is to be found in political "leadership."
The motivation here is to climb on the bandwagon of labor
union popularity in order to get elected to office. Sympathy?
Hardly!

As a novelist says of· one of these characters, "He had
learned to love the poor, *profitably!*"

Minimum wage laws generally call to mind only those leg-
islative edicts bearing the label. In 1938 the minimum was

---

[1]Gunnar Myrdal, *The American Dilemma,* New York, rev. ed. 1962.

25 cents; in 1945, 40 cents; and since has risen step by step to $1.60. The pressure is on to raise it again. These edicts, however, are only the obvious. Every arbitrary wage coercively imposed by labor unions, over and above whatever the free market wage would be, is really a minimum wage. The minimum wage for a captain of a 747 jet is $57,000 annually. Try to get the job for less! But stop not here. The tariff and all other restrictions to free and unfettered exchanges are, in a strict economic sense, minimum wage laws. Those who condemn minimum wage laws, so-called, and lend support to other infractions of the free market such as wage and price controls are proclaiming their inconsistency. In every case these fixities and rigidities—these closures of the market— wreak their hardship on consumers; and the poorer the person, the greater the hardship!

What is the alternative? What advice shall we give the person who earnestly desires to help "the poor?"

GIVE HIM RESPECT

First of all, he must recognize and respect as an individual the one he would love—which means to encourage but in no way to interfere with that person's capacity, will, and effort to help himself. In other words, afford him every opportunity to *earn* his way. How earn it? By serving others, of course. How else does anyone *earn* anything! And what is the most likely opportunity for a poor man to earn his way? By selling his services to the highest bidder in open competition. Let buyers compete for his services—which means, in general, that the highest bidder will be the employer who can most profitably use that person's services. That employer will earn a profit, not because he is exploiting anyone, but because he is most efficiently using scarce resources for purposes that consumers want and can afford. And "the poor" will reap benefits both as employees and consumers as they move upward out of poverty.

The question is this: how can these countless thousands in the labor union and political categories so flagrantly abuse the poor and be applauded rather than condemned for their actions? The answer is that labor union people and politicians who sponsor this nonsense are doing precisely what most citizens believe to be right. The overwhelming majority of citizens, operating on good intentions, fail to recognize that impediments in the market must frustrate their objective. Were the consensus free-market oriented, the political meddlers would not get to first base with their schemes; they would be thrown out of office.

LAISSEZ FAIRE

The next question is, what shall be done to bring more light into this darkness? Perhaps it boils down to this: more individuals than now learning to respect the *preferences* of others as well as their own. If I prefer to wait on table for $1.00 an hour, why should not this disposition on my part be as much honored as that of another who prefers to be President of the U.S.A.? Maybe you prefer teaching for the sheer joy of it—psychic gain—to running a cannery where you might make a fortune—monetary gain. I say, blessings on you and on all others whatever their preferences, so long as you and they are peaceful. This is no more than simple justice, and anyone who acts to the contrary dons the robes of a dictator, intending to run the lives of others.

This simple justice and the aforementioned simple facts would seem to be within the grasp and the practice of a majority of citizens. It is my contention that these are attainable achievements in the moral and economic realm. By and large, however, they are not attained. Why? What is the impediment that hinders us from actually attaining the ends which in fact are within our power to attain? A priceless answer if it can be discovered! Let me share a thought that is becoming more and more a conviction. The essence of this thought was expressed by Ralph Waldo Emerson:

> We lie in the lap of immense intelligence, which makes us receivers of its truth and organs of its activity. When we discern justice, when we discern truth, we do nothing of ourselves, but *allow a passage of its beams.* (Italics added)

I have quoted this before, certain that it expressed an important truth. However, it took the remarks of a recent acquaintance to help me realize its full meaning. This individual, as we met for the first time, acknowledged how helpful my writings had been, and then added, pointing to the head, "It is all here. You have merely helped me put together and to better understand that which is already within me." This is an insight that rivals Emerson's!

Emerson's point now seems clear to me and it helps to explain what stands between the attainable and its attainment: a failure to realize one's potential or an unwillingness to discover and to heed the truths within.

As Emerson so eloquently phrases it, we do, indeed, "lie in the lap of an immense intelligence." As with all radiant energy, this intelligence is in constant movement and it flows through all life. The problem of gaining understanding is one of arresting "its beams," of intercepting or appropriating that which already is within us or is passing through us.

We can be helpful to one another, not by posing as this intelligence but by using, expressing, sharing such of this mysterious energy as we may be fortunate enough to intercept. Once this way to enlightenment is perceived and practiced—a near reversal of present methods—then we may befriend the poor, not merely in proclaimed intentions but in reality. Our hearts and heads will be working in harmony.

8

DESPOTIC AND HYPOTHETIC AUTHORITY

Fame is no sure test of merit.
—CARLYLE

According to one authority, "Acceptable Authority is a power that cannot be *intelligently* or *reasonably* questioned."[1] Questionable authority, then, would be that which is slavishly feared or blindly worshiped.

Nearly everyone is aware of and rightly fears despotic authority—the arbitrary rule of life coercively imposed by some on others. Fending it off—its riddance—is one of the major problems of our time.

Troublesome as is despotic authority, I am beginning to suspect that hypothetic authority may represent an even greater threat to our well-being. This brand of authority is not imposed on me by others but, instead, is supposed by me to be an attribute of others. Unless my critical faculties are alert, I may regard many others as authorities on all things

---

[1]Felix Morley, *The Power in the People,* Princeton, N.J., 1949, p. 131.

because of their outstanding skills and knowledge about some things. Because of their seeming credentials—academic degrees, titles, fame or notoriety, prestige, and so on—the inclination is to hypothesize omnicompetence. They are regarded as the last and final word—authority—not only in areas where they are expert but also in areas where they may be totally lacking in competence.

Despotic authority coercively pushes us into endeavors not consonant with our uniqueness and, conversely, it keeps us from endeavors which might effectively utilize our real talents. Potential musical geniuses forced to work in the sputnik factory, for instance! Hypothetic authority, on the other hand, has no push to it at all. Instead, it is of our own making, consisting of conclusions or inferences we ourselves draw. These suppositions when wrong may lead us more astray than do the coercive impositions.

CELEBRITY ENDORSEMENTS

Our unawareness in this respect is assumed to be so general that we witness constant attempts to exploit it: famous band leaders, baseball stars, actors, and other prestigious persons singing the praises of motor cars, breakfast foods, sleeping powders, cigarettes, and what have you. These celebrities come before us not because they have a product knowledge they can hardly wait to share but because of a handsome stipend. The handsome stipend, one may acknowledge, depends in part upon an urge among consumers to know what the stars are driving, eating, sleeping with, smoking and doing generally. The stipend also depends largely upon the producer's ability to supply a good product for the star's endorsement. Consumers do not like to be fooled.

However, in this area of goods and services, the consumer can never be "taken in" for long. Pure self-interest in day-to-day living with the simple things of life steers him clear of fakery no matter how cleverly devised. Sooner or later advertisers will awaken to how wide awake consumers are. No problem here!

The danger looms when we move from the things by which we daily sustain ourselves—things close to our hides—to the theories and precepts that make these things possible. It is when we shift from personal economy to the structures of political economy that hypothetic authority so often leads us astray. We may not be impressed unduly by a star reading a prepared script concerning the virtues of a product about which he knows next to nothing, but we are easily "taken in" by a scientist, for instance, writing an article or book about which we know little, if anything.

A RADICAL DEPARTURE

A case in point: I have read several books by a famous zoologist. He impresses me as an outstanding authority in his field. Only once, in those of his books I have read, does he veer from the discipline in which he appears to be so knowledgeable:

Throughout human history until recent times, most human beings died in infancy, and no more than a very small percentage survived to ripe old age, carrying with them the wisdom of their experience or the foolishness of their years. Now all is changing, thanks to antibodies, antibiotics, the surgeons' knife, and *the welfare state.* (Italics added)[2]

Now suppose that I had no awareness of the welfare state's utter fallacy, founded as it is on despotic authority. Favorably impressed by this author's skills in zoology, how easy it would be for me to hypothesize his authority as a political economist —to be "taken in"! After all, he affirms what most politicians are saying and many Americans are believing. In this instance, however, I was saved from error because he veered into my area of thought.

Albert Einstein, perhaps the most renowned mathematician who ever lived, sided with despotic authority: he embraced socialism. It is impossible to reckon the number of people who hypothesized his authority in an area in which I believe he had no competence.

Dr. Alexis Carrel, a noted physician, wrote a famous book, *Man, The Unknown.* I read it in 1935, before I had thought much about the freedom philosophy. He so skillfully criticized our societal ills—all criticisms agreeable to me—that I swallowed his remedies without a quibble. He easily sold me "a bill of goods." Because of my carelessness, my lack of alertness, I assigned to him a hypothetic authority. Not until rereading the book years later did I recognize his conclusion as despotic authority.

Perhaps these examples are sufficient for illustrative purposes. Examples abound on every hand and by the tens of

---

[2]N. J. Berrill, *Inherit the Earth,* New York, 1966, p. 181.

thousands. There are two questions to answer: (1) Why is hypothetic authority more dangerous than despotic authority? and (2) Is there a simple way to avoid this error?

HOW AVOID DECEPTION?

I have observed that we have no reason to concern ourselves about consumers being victimized by "Madison Avenue." True, we have many professional worrycrats who do so concern themselves but, really, who is "taken in"! You? Never! It is always someone else; yet, try to find that person! At the food, fiber, and gadgetry level the consumer is way ahead of both producers and advertisers. Self-paying customers possess a commendable "show me" attitude.

But fundamental to an abundance of food, fiber, and gadgetry is the societal framework, that is, how human relations are structured. Montesquieu put it in a simple sentence: "A country is well cultivated not because it is fertile but because it is free." Russia is as fertile as the U.S.A. but not as free. No need to labor this point.

Whether a country is free or not depends upon the consensus. If a majority of a country's people give lip service to the planned economy and the welfare state—socialism—that is precisely what will prevail. There will not, cannot, be an abundance of food, fiber, gadgetry. I am unaware of any historical instance to refute this.

Hypothetic authority, now on the rampage, substantially contributes to the current consensus favoring despotic authority. Briefly, the former lies at the root of the latter. Consumers who are so alert at the surface manifestations of freedom are, for the most part, cutting away the roots of abundant subsistence; they are innocently contributing to scarcity, thwarting their own interests. Although producers and advertisers cannot fool them overmuch at the goods and services level, consumers are easily "taken in" at the theoretical and conceptual level.

I will readily concede that an individual, unless giving profound attention to social and economic theories and practices, has only a dim chance of avoiding the error here in question. Life is so complex that, seemingly, we must rely on other people's word for most things, for each of us does, in fact, live off others. And who better to follow than one who is prestigiously positioned! If he be an expert in astronomy, why not rely on him in political economy!

CHOOSE A SOUND PREMISE

There must be some formula by which the error so common to hypothetic authority can be avoided. The simplest way I have found is to adopt for self a basic premise, that is, a fundamental point of reference from which one's position can be readily established on a host of matters. My own premise is my answer to the question, what is man's earthly purpose? The answer that comes through loud and clear to me is: Individual growth, development, emergence, evolution along the lines of one's creative uniqueness.

How does one employ this technique? Merely check all ideas—one's own or anyone else's—with the premise. If an idea is perceived as thwarting this aim, cast it aside; never embrace it. If, on the other hand, an idea is in harmony with this high purpose—promotive of it—then embrace it; stand in its favor. If one's premise be sound and if one reasons logically from it—deductively—then one's positions will always be sound, the dangers of hypothetic authority avoided.

As to a premise, frame one that can proudly be pronounced before God and man alike. Make certain that it is free from all traces of despotic authority, which is to say, a premise founded on individual liberty. Thus armed, one can search for truth from all sources without fear of being "taken in." Practiced a bit, this method of thinking will soon become habitual, natural, an intellectual way of life.

9

GREAT OR CELEBRATED?

If any man seeks for greatness, let him forget greatness and ask for truth, and he will find both.
—HORACE MANN

Many years ago a prestigious national weekly carried a section headed, "The Great and the Near Great." I have often thought it should have been entitled "The Celebrated and the Also Rans." For, in my judgment, most of the personalities reviewed were only celebrated and not great. There is a marked distinction between these two terms, and the failure to note the difference leads to mischief.

The celebrated person: "famous; renowned; well-publicized." The great man: "having or showing nobility of mind, purpose, etc."

True, numerous great men are also famous or celebrated, but the number must be legion of celebrated men who bear no earmarks of greatness. For instance, I would refer to Goethe as both great and celebrated, and to Stalin, Hitler, and a thousand and one others as celebrated but not great.

When renown is mistaken for greatness people are led astray; they are likely to believe that the sole way to be great is to be celebrated. This tends to deflect the eye from what constitutes greatness and persuades men to strive for fame rather than nobility of mind. I firmly believe that many of the greatest men who have ever lived or who live today are unknown to you or me. Except among intimate acquaintances, we are only aware of celebrities, a few of whom may be great but not the greatest.

Let us reflect first on the celebrity syndrome. Aside from the false notion that fame and greatness are synonymous and therefore renown must be a worthy aim, what else spurs men to seek popularity? Mere acclaim by the masses would not seem to be drive enough by itself to take possession of a normal person; there must be a companion failure of the mind. What might it be? Egomania—a passion for center stage—in a word, pride!

When it comes to man fulfilling life's higher goals—"nobility of mind, purpose, etc."—an inflated ego is doubtless more dangerous—damaging—than high blood pressure. Thus, this should be guarded against.

What accounts for this type of inflation? Thoughtlessness, of course—no reasoned barrier standing against the ego's wild growth.

BEWARE OF PRAISE

This hankering for praise and adulation is indeed heady stuff—so believable! True, I find myself praising others and, on occasion, someone praises me. It is not praise that is in error but, rather, one's inability to pigeonhole it, to realize that the praise is not the accomplishment itself. Here am I, distraught by lack of achievement and along comes a letter telling me how wonderful I am. I have not advanced one whit in accomplishment, but self-esteem takes a mighty leap forward. What a great man am I! You see, I make the mistake of thinking of myself as great when, in fact, only my renown has inched ahead—slightly celebrated.

The cure for this? Be neither exalted by praise nor distraught by criticism. Let praise or adulation pass by as a refreshing breeze. And let criticism be examined for whatever truth can be found in it.

THE GREATEST IS UNKNOWN

I recall lunching with several scholarly individuals, one of those friendly affairs where the talk may take any turn. On this occasion, the greatest American was the issue. Only Washington, Jefferson, Hamilton, and Lincoln were in the contest for first place. Settle on one of these, they seemed to think, and there stands the greatest! True, all four qualify as great, but the talk was confined to them simply because they rank high among this nation's celebrities. After listening for an hour, I made my first remark: "The greatest American is someone whom no one at this table ever heard of." I demonstrated this by mentioning several men in politics and business currently most highly publicized, and who a century hence will be among the celebrities of our time. I added; "Each of you thinks of yourself as greater than any of these." They agreed, and for good and sufficient reason!

To be celebrated requires no more than notoriety—"taken note of." We take note of weeds as well as roses, and frequently pay more attention to men who are outstandingly depraved than to those who stand out as geniuses. Nobility of mind is the criterion for greatness, but fame may be extended to scoundrels.

What are the grounds for claiming that the greatest men are not known to any one of us? For the simple reason that the noblest minds are beyond our powers of perception. This is to say that there are those whose conscience and consciousness are so elevated that we are unable to take note of them. Beyond our ken! Incredible? No; our own experiences, if reflected upon, attest to this fact.

For instance, a person who grows in awareness comes upon thoughts each day that are brand new to him. He may have read the words before without grasping the meaning. Why should we conclude that what we are able to perceive today is the limit of our perceptive ability? The notion that I now know it all is utterly naive, a denial of an infinite unknown. If today I perceive a person's thought to which yesterday I was blind, why not be certain that tomorrow holds the same promise? And, further, why not carry this observation to its logical conclusion by frankly admitting that there have been and are individuals whose nobility of mind is beyond one's comprehension?

OVERSOULS

These oversouls to whom I refer—not Yogis in Himalayan caves—whose thoughts are unknown may be on a first-name basis with us. They could be from any walk of life and are not associated with fame, fortune, rank, age, formal education, race, creed, color. Possibly, your maid or next door neighbor! We do not know because we cannot know.

Doubtless, the greatest individuals are, to some extent, in communion with Intelligences about which we are but dimly aware. These persons are not in communion with others because what they perceive is of an order beyond their powers of communication.

If all of this seems esoteric or "ivory tower," reflect on a current phenomenon, the little book, *Jonathan Livingston Seagull,* by Richard Bach. The author disclaims any credit, for he frankly confesses that the idea came to him as a flash of enlightenment and the words flowed from his typewriter as in automatic writing—a force at work which neither he nor anyone else understands. The book is sweeping this and other countries, certainly one of the best sellers of all time.

Here we observe the voice of an Intelligence which Bach, left to his own resources, would never have been able to communicate to others. In this instance, however, communicable words accompanied the insight or intuitive flash, call it what you will.

Richard Bach, an aviator and writer for aviation magazines, could have been described as many of us: neither great nor celebrated. A flash of enlightenment—nobility of mind—beyond his or our comprehension, made him great. Today, he is both celebrated and great.

Let us not overlook the real significance of *Jonathan.* What is the meaning of its phenomenal acceptance? It proves beyond a shadow of a doubt that millions of people are reaching, searching for the sublime, for what we are not yet. This parable is a loud and clear demonstration of the possible: a moral and spiritual renaissance rooted in greatness. If we heed its message and aim for nobility of mind—not renown— we will be on the only path there is toward greatness.

10

THE LAW OF
ACTION AND REACTION

Walk while ye have the light, lest
darkness come upon you.
—JOHN 12:35

Up and down, back and forth, rise and fall; these movements mark the course of civilizations. A "renaissance" followed by a "dark age"; a period of enlightenment and then a decline from grace. Evolution, devolution, evolution, devolution, on and on—action and reaction—a sequence to be found in the future as the past. Why? It is ordained by Nature's pattern; it is phased into the Cosmic Order.

If this be a correct assessment, it might seem to follow that all work aimed at a better world is fruitless—tilting at windmills, contesting against the inevitable. A second thought, however, reveals that intelligent effort can cause evolution to inch ahead over time; the ascents longer, the declines less precipitous. While action and reaction will persist, it is undeniably within man's power to cause this sequence to operate at higher and higher levels. This is to say that it can be made to rise from the low and ignoble to the high and noble, from the dog-eat-dog to the Golden Rule way of life.

Of course, there is no point in examining this hope unless we believe that action and reaction—the law of polarity or tension of the opposites—are forever in play, that societal events are shaped by how each of us acts and reacts. Emerson, the philosopher, put it clearly and beautifully:

> *Polarity,* or action and reaction, we meet in every part of nature; in darkness and light; in heat and cold; in the ebb and flow of waters; in male and female; in the inspiration and expiration of plants and animals; in the systole and diastole of the heart; in the undulations of fluids and of sound; in the centrifugal and centripetal gravity;. . . . If the south attracts, the north repels. . . . An inevitable dualism bisects nature, so that each thing is a half, and suggests another thing to make it whole; as spirit, matter; man, woman; subjective, objective; in, out; upper, under; motion, rest; yea, nay.[1]

For scientific support of this idea, refer to Robert A. Millikan, renowned physicist and Nobel Prize winner for his measurement of the electrical charge of the electron:

> All atoms are built up out of definite numbers of positive and negative electrons. All chemical forces are due to the attractions of positive for negative electrons. *All elastic forces are due to the attractions and repulsions of electrons.*[2]

---

[1]Newton Dillaway, *The Gospel of Emerson,* Lee's Summit, Missouri, 1949, p. 71.

[2]*Encyclopaedia Britannica,* 1943, Vol. VIII, p. 340.

Salute the American flag. That arm in motion is as perfect an example of elasticity as is a wagging tongue, a smile, or a raising of an eyebrow. What goes on here? These and all elasticities can be traced to the attractions and repulsions—actions and reactions—of electrons within tiny atoms! What lies back of the interactions of the electrons? The cortex or diencephalon, of course. How does the mind cause the electrons to respond? About this we know nothing except that the decision to salute the flag was a reaction to preceding actions, difficult to identify. We believe that "an inevitable dualism bisects nature"—all of it!

THE MORAL CODE

The thesis I am about to offer is an ancient one. Abbreviated and rephrased, the Mosaic law proclaims:

> God promises to the people of Israel that if they obey his moral and civil laws—righteous actions—they will be blessed with material abundance. But he warns that this very blessing can serve as a snare. If they forget the source they will exalt themselves thus: "My power and the might of mine hand hath gotten me this wealth." God then promises the inevitable reaction against man's false claims of divinity: "I testify against you this day that ye shall surely perish."[3]

About a thousand years later the promised reaction to moral action was phrased, "Seek ye first the Kingdom of God and his Righteousness, and *these things* shall be added unto you." This is to say that when a people put truth and right-

---

[3]Deuteronomy 8:6-20.

eousness first and foremost, the dividends—things—follow as a matter of course. The implication is clear: seek first "these things" and neither truth nor things will be forthcoming.

Today does not differ from ages past. The reaction to moral action is the affluent life; and the usual, unthinking reaction to affluence is a disregard of moral action and the subsequent decline and fall. This is the historical pattern; we are witnessing the common sequence in the U.S.A. today.

Reflect on the millions of Americans living today in affluence beyond the dreams of any other people at any other time. But note how few there are who have the slightest awareness of source. They seem to think that all of this is their due, automatically, for merely being alive. The hard and sobering fact? All of this array of gadgetry—dishwashers, autos, telephones, air transportation, electric lighting and heating—is beyond their ken. There is not one among those countless items that any living person knows how to make. Yet, most Americans are thinking, if not saying, what man long ago was warned against, "My power and the might of mine hand hath gotten me this wealth." They have lost sight of the fact that all of "these things" have resulted from the knowledge and practice of difficult human virtues. These things are but dividends—reactions—in response to righteous action.

AFLAME WITH RIGHTEOUSNESS

Tocqueville, trying to discover the miracle of America—searching for the root cause of this phenomenon—gave the best answer known to me: "I found them aflame with righteousness. America is great because America is good. When America ceases to be good, America will cease to be great."

No person can even begin to list, let alone document, the actions and reactions that led to the righteousness—the morality that featured the America Tocqueville examined. Nor is a knowledge of the countless, diverse details necessary. We need only know (1) that righteousness was the source of our affluence, (2) that, by and large, the source is all but forgotten, (3) that, as forewarned, disaster awaits this unawareness, and (4) that we must re-acknowledge and honor the source, or surely perish.

It is obvious that the reaction to affluence, if not scrupulously guarded against, is the exaltation of self and claims of divinity: "My power and the might of mine hand has gotten me this wealth." Only now and then do we observe an affluent individual who has the good sense to work and think and grow as do those who have no choice but "to root hog or die." The normal reaction to affluence is nonuse and atrophy of the faculties, as if man's purpose were to get out of rather than into life, that is, to fatten, vegetate, retire!

AN IMMUTABLE LAW

Bear in mind that we are dealing with an immutable law, that is, a law that cannot be modified by wishing. So far as our own power is concerned, it can only be applied on the terms by which this law operates. If we do not exert this power, the law will continue to operate as in the past: evolution, devolution, evolution, devolution, on and on.

An example of the law's normal operation comes to mind: Our Pilgrim Fathers, in the first three years after landing at Plymouth Rock, lived in accord with communistic notions: from each according to ability, to each according to *need.* Regardless of their religious sincerity, theirs was not a righteous way of life. The result? Starvation! The reaction? Some hard-headed thinking: to each according to *his own production!* The reaction to this right thinking over the following three centuries? The greatest outburst of creative energy ever known! As the Roman, Horace, observed about 2,000 years ago:

> Adversity has the effect of eliciting talents which in prosperous circumstances would have lain dormant.

Must we await adversity and the reaction that will follow —perhaps in decades, or even centuries? That is the relevant question. While the past may well repeat itself, that does not *necessarily* follow. The outcome depends exclusively on the degree of consistency—men's willingness to conform to principle in practice—that can be brought to bear on the present.

As I see it, the usual reaction to affluence is to fall asleep so far as life's higher purposes are concerned—"wealth accumulates and men decay." According to the historical pattern, the only alarm clock has been disaster—adversity. This is an absurd neglect of our powers. *Why not awaken ourselves!* We need only to sharpen our perceptions to see the adversity in the offing and then to react as if it were already upon us. Behave as we would—work, think, grow— were it really a case of "root hog or die"! Use the affluence we still have to sharpen our perceptions. Let us recognize that wealth is a tool that makes enlightenment easier; it frees us from the obstacles—the slavery—which adversity imposes.

This, in my view, is the only way to cause the law of action and reaction to operate above the dog-eat-dog level and at the Golden Rule level.

11

THE RIGHT I OWE YOU

Man precedes the State, and possesses, prior to the formation of any State, the right of providing for the sustenance of his body.

—POPE LEO XIII

The several billions of us now inhabiting the globe are members respectively of some clan, tribe, or nation. An important question: What right does each of us owe any or every other?

You have the right to do with yourself and your own whatever you please so long as your pursuits—noble or ignoble—do no injury to me and mine. In this respect, you have no responsibility for me nor I for you; let the outcome in either case be what it may. At most, in such personal pursuits, we can be the source of each other's disappointment or admiration. In this strictly individualistic sense, I owe you nothing more than noninterference; all else in solitude I owe to myself.

Life, however, is not accomplished strictly in solitude, nor can it be. We live both in solitude and in society. So the problem of rights concerns not merely the *I* but the *we* as well. My purpose here is to look beyond my right in solitude to my rights in society—civil rights, the kind we define by civil law. In brief, what are your claims on me? In logic and justice, they must be identical to my claims on you. So, what is it that I owe you—and vice versa?[1]

The answer to this question is of prime importance. For we have now in the 20th century strayed so far from reason that mere wishes are regarded as rights. Examples: we wish for a decent standard of living without working; we wish to be paid for not farming; we wish that employers be forced to pay whatever wages we demand; we wish for a Gateway Arch; we wish to be protected against competitors while insisting that our suppliers be competitive; we wish for renewal of our dying community. These and thousands of other wishes are now incorporated into the civil law as rights.[2]

AHEAD LIES DISASTER

Sober reflection reveals where this wild interpretation of rights is taking us: (1) governmental costs soaring billions of dollars annually beyond what can be collected by direct tax levies, (2) monetary inflation as a means of syphoning private property into the coffers of government, (3) rising

---

[1] I do not mean to exclude the practice of Judeo-Christian charity. Here my reference is only to civil law having to do with legal claims. Charity has to do with morality and mercy, not legality and justice.

[2] See my, "When Wishes Become Rights," *The Freeman*, November 1964.

prices, (4) wage and price controls. Unless this whole political scheme is abolished, rationing must inevitably follow
and then the total state—an end to freedom in America.

What, pray tell, accounts for our disastrous behavior?
Perhaps we shall never know for certain, because cause un-
derlies cause ad infinitum. The causes we can perceive lie
near the surface, and the most obvious one in this case is a
habit into which so many people have fallen: collectivistic
thinking. Or, a better term might be lump thinking: farmers
have "rights"; states and cities have "rights"; blacks have
"rights"; the have-nots have "rights"; laborers have "rights";
consumers have "rights"; on and on. The individual person
is forgotten as lump thinking turns thoughtless citizens into
voting blocs, a process encouraged by the politician because it economizes his manipulative efforts.

Correction of this tendency requires recognition of a simple
truth: *only the individual has rights.* It is exclusively the individual who experiences justice or injustice, who evidences
morality or immorality, who gains or loses, speaks, thinks,
prays, hates, loves, lies, cheats, reasons, practices integrity,
has feelings. The collective, no matter how you lump it, has
neither mind nor conscience, nor any other personal attribute
—not one!

THE MADNESS OF CROWDS

A crowd does not, cannot, reason. It is self-evident that
only the individuals within the crowd have brains and thus
possess such powers. "Mob psychology" is simply the irrational mental state of individuals who attempt to transfer

personal responsibility to a fictitious entity—the crowd. A mere category, such as labor, is personified, and so are businessmen, and we get Labor and Business. Or Medicine, the Law, and so on.

This, I believe, helps explain the absence of reason, the double talk, the flight from integrity, the utter nonsense characteristic of much political talk. Reasoning with something that cannot reason—Labor and Business, for instance—is out of the question. The politician who falls into the error of thinking of us as blocs addresses himself to "bloc-heads," not to individuals. Is it any wonder that the process persuades men to regard wishes as rights!

As to the rights of each person, rationality requires that we drop all of the collectivistic jargon; it makes no sense—none whatsoever! With this done, there we stand not as a mass but as millions of discrete individuals, each a little world unto himself, each entitled to precisely the same right as any of the others, all equal in every respect before the civil law. Rationally, discrimination is not admissible.

Now, then, what is it that you as one of these millions owe me and all the others? Exactly what I owe you, whoever you may be: *the opportunity,* without let or hindrance, to go as far creatively as your aspirations and talents will permit! This is what I owe you—no more no less.

12

RESTRAINT OR RELEASE?

None are more hopelessly enslaved
than those who falsely believe they
are free.

—GOETHE

Two diametrically opposed ways of life are implicit in this question. Put simply, the choice is between slavery or freedom. "To be or not to be," to become or to be overcome is the issue here at stake.

For some years I have been defining freedom as "no man-concocted *restraints* against the *release* of creative human energy." So far, I have received neither approval nor disapproval from any listener or reader. Two inferences can be deduced from this silence: (1) complete agreement or (2) too vague an understanding of what this definition means to evoke a response. More than likely it is the latter, for generalities—even when carefully phrased—seldom stimulate either approbation or opprobrium. The tendency is to let them stand for what they are: pleasant and noncontroversial bits of verbiage—mere words or meaningless images!

An example: "Ye shall know the truth, and the truth shall make you free." This is often quoted, but who really understands or questions its meaning? It is a Biblical pleasantry and scarcely anyone, regardless of ideological or philosophical leanings, bothers to look behind the words. Who does not wish to be free or to know the truth! Similarly, who would not prefer release to restraint!

Simplification, I have discovered, is more likely to be achieved by explanation than by brevity. "No man-concocted restraints against the release of creative human energy" is brief enough but it fails to simplify; it does not explain and, thus, I fear, is not much understood.

To be or not to be—to become what is within one's potential or to be overcome at some stagnation level—is, as I see it, the prime human problem.

> . . . the universal power is ever effecting release, freedom. . . . This key is found in learning the art of ascension, of lifting the consciousness . . . . any person who flows as life flows has solved the problem of human existence. With serious obstructions, we fade and die.[1]

Stated another way, serious restraints are deadly.

PSYCHOLOGICAL AND SOCIOLOGICAL RESTRAINTS

Man-concocted restraints fall into two categories: psychological and sociological. Restraints of the former variety are the kind an individual inherits or imposes upon himself; the

---

[1]Selections from *Consent* by Newton Dillaway, *op. cit.*

latter are what others impose upon him. Far more attention is given to the latter than to the former, simply because restraints by others are more easily detected than those existing in self. It is so much easier to detect the faults of others than one's own. Social restraints may be vicious, of course, but probably are less damaging than the personal taboos and habits from which we fail to release ourselves.

The heart-warming account of the lioness, filmed as "Born Free," comes to mind. That remarkable creature flowed with life from an instinctive, not a rational, direction. Man, as Gerald Heard suggests, has lost many of the instincts that guide the animals and, unfortunately, has not, by and large, acquired or developed that human uniqueness—the power to reason and choose—on which his ascension, the lifting of consciousness—depends. It might be said that we are, with few exceptions, neither animal nor true man. Only rarely is there a person who has significantly bridged the gap. Support for this observation is to be found in contrasting wolves with men. A wolf never kills a wolf; men do kill each other.[2] Or note how so many of us have come to hate evil so much that we forget to love good.

"A thinking reed," Pascal called man. No individual who refuses to think for himself has bridged the gap; he has not yet arrived at that level which distinguishes human uniqueness! A recent experience, typical of our time in history, portrays my point:

---

[2]See "Morals and Weapons" in *King Solomon's Ring* by Konrad Z. Lorenz, New York, 1961, pp. 181-199; also *Never Cry Wolf* by Farley Mowat, New York, 1963.

I overheard the pretty, blond stewardess indignantly explaining to her helpmate that she had just paid 77 cents for a package of cigarettes. "Of all things!"

When I asked how she would feel if she had to pay $77 or $770 for a package of cigarettes, she gave me a withering glance.

I then took from my billfold two pieces of Brazil's paper money, a 50 cruziero note of 1940 vintage and one of today's 10,000 cruziero notes, pointing out that the former was worth seven dollars in 1940 while the latter now is worth $1.60, despite the fact that the dollar has lost 67 per cent of its purchasing value in this period. Had the U.S. dollar depreciated as rapidly as the cruziero, the package of cigarettes she might have purchased for 20 cents in 1940 would cost some 3,500 times as much today!

Anyway, the stewardess exclaimed, "I do not want to think about such things; they are too depressing." This remark calls to mind the ostrich-like behavior of ever so many "leaders" whether in business, politics, labor, religion, education, or whatever—a refusal to think: telltale evidence of refusal to live up to the human level!

LIFTING THE CONSCIOUSNESS

There is another bit of evidence pointing in the same direction: the widely held "conviction" that no one else can have achieved intellectual and spiritual experiences higher than one's own. "Lifting the consciousness"—"the art of ascension"—is, I feel certain, limitless in possibilities. There are reports of experiences by men throughout recorded history that

I personally have not had and do not expect to encounter. Yet, my limited capacity is no ground for doubting that others have gone far beyond me. Insight and intuition are of enormous variety and expansibility. Newton Dillaway writes:

> I had acquired the intuitive knack of taking a book and turning directly to the page that held something I needed to fill out the unfolding Idea.[3]

Richard Bach, as previously related, found the words of *Jonathan Livingston Seagull,* flowing automatically.[4] Many authors and composers have left accounts of the creative process, as they have experienced it.[5]

Most people to whom these phenomena have never happened will refer to them as "mystic stuff" and unbelievable. Well, I have had numerous minor experiences such as Dillaway and Bach describe and, thus, I do believe that others can have experiences that will never happen to me.

To tie the phenomena of the world down to one's own experiences is restraint of the first order. It blocks both inspiration and aspiration. Release is the need.

A state of unconsciousness—that is, not thinking for self—and blindness to the fact that others have intellectual and spiritual experiences beyond one's own are but two among countless restraints of the psyche. Release—freedom from these—is essential before it is possible to become truly human.

Reflect on the variety of shortcomings inherited by each

---

[3]*Consent, op. cit.,* pp. 11.

[4]Richard Bach, *Jonathan Livingston Seagull,* New York, 1972.

[5]Brewster Ghiselin, ed., *The Creative Process,* Berkeley, 1954.

one of us. Add to these the unfavorable situations into which so many are born, environmental impressions or depressions —domineering and the like—which plant their seeds in babyhood and on through adolescence. Genetic and environmental influences, with but rare exceptions, make persons what they are; or, negatively, they tend to keep people from becoming what they might be. Hopelessly tied down to inheritance and environment? Not necessarily!

ATTAINING ADULTHOOD

Dr. Thomas A. Harris, psychiatrist, uses the term "Adulthood" to suggest his answer. Adulthood—always with a capital A—in his sense, is unrelated to age. Actually, it has to do with the art of becoming truly human, of raising the consciousness, of ascension. He tries to demonstrate that it is possible for the individual to shake off these loosely built-in setbacks, to become the captain of his own soul, to *release* himself from the numerous psychological restraints.[6]

Most of the above is my phrasing, not his. And so is this conclusion: *Release begins the moment one starts thinking for self.* Nor need one go to a psychiatrist to do this; merely consult one's own mind! That is easily accessible and the price is right!

The final aim, "no man-concocted restraints against the release of creative human energy" has, as I am attempting to suggest, a dual application; it refers (1) to the psyche and (2) to society. Many of us—devotees of the freedom philos-

---

[6]Thomas A. Harris, *I'm OK—You're OK,* New York, 1969.

ophy—have done much thinking and writing about the latter, but we have paid too little attention to the former. We have been portraying the societal ideal while neglecting its composite parts—individuals and their personal growth. This, however, dwells more upon the faults of others than upon our own.

Let me hasten to add that spelling out the ideal for society is not to be sold short. For, unless the ideal is known, we have nothing at which to aim. The societal ideal, as I see it, is simple enough: relegate organized force—government—to codifying and enforcing the taboos, the destructive actions such as violence, fraud, predation, misrepresentation, and the like.

SELF-DISCIPLINE

Unfortunately, there is nothing in the nature of government that enables it to curb its tendency to grow at the expense of the individual. If there is to be any limitation upon government, it must be developed in such a way that it does not call for additional governmental activity; in other words, it must be expressed personally and voluntarily in the form of self-discipline. What this means is self-improvement, self-responsibility, self-respect of such high order that one is not tempted to covet his neighbor's success, or even to subsidize—and thereby aggravate—his neighbor's alleged ignorance or poverty or other defect of character.

In a word, mind one's own business. Leave all creative activities—no exceptions—to men acting freely, voluntarily, privately, competitively, cooperatively. This would release us from restraints by others, a situation in which we would like to find ourselves, to which we aspire.

However—and this is the rub—the societal ideal is not even remotely within reach except as there be a goodly number of individuals capable of reaching "Adulthood." This is to say that no one may hope to release himself from the restraints imposed by others who has not succeeded to some extent in releasing himself from his own inner restraints. No plum pudding can be made of mudballs.

Men who fail to think may expect to find themselves in a bad society. A good society is possible only among those who have reached the human level of thinking for themselves.

13

TWO WAYS OF
LIVING OFF OTHERS

*Dark Error's other hidden side is
truth.*

—VICTOR HUGO

Suppose the earth were uninhabited and a single human being dropped onto it. He would perish in short order, for man
is at once an individualistic and a social being. He lives both
in solitariness and in society—with himself and with others—
and cannot exist under one condition without the other. As-
suredly, he cannot survive as a lone human being.

We live off each other; and the more advanced the society,
that is, the more specialized, the more pronounced is this
interdependence. I, for instance, devote my efforts to writing
and lecturing. Obviously, I could not support myself by these
efforts alone—I count on the cooperation of others. When it
comes to subsistence, I live off others and so does everyone
else. I make but an infinitesimal fraction of the things on
which my life depends; indeed, I do not know how to produce
many of those other things.

There are two ways—and only two—of living off others: free exchange on the one hand or coerced exchange on the other. The distinction is between trading and taking, which is to say between two-party assent and one-party dissent—as in robbery, for instance.

THE PROBLEM OF BEING PRACTICAL

Nearly everyone will agree to the rightness of the first way and to the evil of the second when phrased in these elementary and simple terms. There is only one honorable way to live off others and that is in free and willing exchange —trade, by which each party gains according to his judgment. Further, most people will share the view that there is no greater evil than living off others by coercion. This, of course, is an ancient truism:

> Sin is not the violation of a law or convention . . . but ignorance . . . which seeks its own private gain at the expense of others.[1]

So far so good, so long as only simple principles are considered. However, in the cold reality of daily affairs, principles are forgotten more often than not; being "practical" allows tiny "buts" to creep in, little exceptions to the rules:

> *But* surely we must take from some and give to others to assure an educated citizenry.
> *But* in an emergency it is necessary that government

---

[1] *The Bhagavadgita,* translated by S. Radhakrishnan, New York, 1948, p. 224.

come to the rescue by taking from the haves and giving to the have-nots.

But everyone must be guaranteed a decent standard of living, and so on and on.

A BROKEN PRINCIPLE

In brief, living off others by a resort to coercion, once condoned, even in minor and exceptional cases, tears the principle asunder; the camel's nose is in the tent; there is no solid ground to stand on. Break the principle and no stopping place remains; logic and reason, right and wrong no longer serve as guides. Lost in a sea of "buts"! Henry Hazlitt refers to the situation as "Welfarism Gone Wild!" Merely observe one item alone: Social welfare expenditures by the Federal government (in millions of dollars):[2]

1935	$ 3,207
1940	3,443
1945	4,399
1950	10,541
1955	14,623
1960	24,957
1965	37,720
1968	60,314
1970	77,321
1971	92,411

This is just one part of the game of living off others by coerced exchange. Note the trend of increased expenditures—

---

[2]See "Welfarism Gone Wild" by Henry Hazlitt, *The Freeman,* May 1972.

29 times as high today as 36 years ago![3] Even worse is the current political pressure to accelerate the trend. And all because the principle was abandoned, the bars let down, to accommodate originally some minor "practicality." We permitted a few "buts" to sneak into our thinking!

SPECIAL PRIVILEGES

Living off others by coercion is not always conducted by the formal agency of government itself. The government sometimes deputizes other organizations with a portion of its coercive power. Every above-market wage rate exacted by labor unions, for example, is precisely of this order. Again, the harm results from admitting a small "but" into our thinking. It went something like this: The common laborer has no chance against wealthy employers; they will exploit the poor fellow. So, to pit economic muscle against economic greed, these poor laborers must unionize and their unions be given coercive power to enforce their demands. In a word, let them live off others by coercion.

Here was a small "but" imposed on our economy to "protect" the little man. Nothing more was originally intended. However, as is easily seen, once we abandon the principle, there is no stopping place. Little man? The process has mushroomed to higher levels. Airline pilots, for instance, coercively exact wages up to $57,000 annually. Throughout com-

---

[3]This figure on a per capita basis and adjusted for the declining dollar (now one-third of its 1939 value) would show a six-fold rather than a 29-fold increase. However, were this trend in expenditures to continue—the inflation pattern—the dollar would, sooner or later, become worthless. Without a trustworthy medium of exchange, the whole economy falls into a shambles.

merce, industry, the professions, the arts—you name it—perhaps 20 million people are thus behaving. Merely bear in mind that every dollar exacted over and beyond what a free market wage would be represents living off others by coercion. It is taking, not trading!

Nor have we here exhausted the list of coercive practices. Examples by the thousands are to be found in most walks of life. My point, however, is not to dwell on these manifest evils; it is, instead, to emphasize the importance of adhering strictly to right principle and never admitting any "buts" in the first place.

Admittedly, many high-minded individuals, overcome by compassion for those they see in unfortunate circumstances, suggest a "but" here and there, a small hole in the dike now and then. Compassion, I insist, must be bound down by the chains of reality. To save those unfortunates by breaking a principle, simply because one cannot see how they otherwise would be saved, is to endanger a whole nation; it is to reduce everyone to a status begging compassion.

If a principle be right then its practice has to be right. Living off others by free and willing exchange is right in principle. Who will not agree to this as against its alternative? Therefore, this principle has to be rewarding in practice. If we cannot envision its practice as the better of the two ways, as the more beneficial to all, let us not abandon the principle but look to the limits of our own vision. Freedom works!

14

JUSTICE VERSUS
SOCIAL JUSTICE

*Justice is to give every man his
own.*

—ARISTOTLE

What is justice? "Justice is the end of government. It is the
end of civil society." This conclusion by James Madison
(Federalist No. 51) also suits me. My contention is that justice and so-called social justice are opposites and that to promote the latter is to retard the former.

Justice, as honesty, is an achievement in conduct relating
to others. True, we can be unjust or dishonest to self, but that
is another matter. The justice of which we speak here is a
societal problem involving a relationship between you and me
and other individuals. Not groups or classes, but only individuals experience justice or injustice, honesty or dishonesty,
harmony or disharmony. We know society is comprised of *I's*
and *You's* but beyond this, "we have not even the remotest
idea of what Society is."[1] Justice cannot be rendered to
everyone in general, only to each one in particular.

---

[1] Jose Ortega y Gasset, *Man and People,* New York, 1963, p. 151.

What we call civil society consists of numerous, diverse, varying individuals, each a world to himself, and living contemporaneously. Each can reach his potential best only as justice prevails in personal relations, that is, in the absence of injustice. Understood in this manner, justice is indeed the end of civil society.

Government in its ideal concept can have no other end than a common justice, for this is the end of civil society of which government is the arm or agent. The Goddess of Justice is blindfolded; if she peeks, she cheats. Her concern is not with what or who the person is, but what he did or is charged with doing. This is the meaning of "A government of laws, not of men."

RULES OF JUSTICE

A fair field and no favor—no special privilege for anyone—admittedly is an objective to be more ardently hoped for than seriously expected. Yet, no move in that direction is possible short of an understanding of what justice is and how it can be rendered. Certain verities may help to bring our ideal into focus.

• *Do not do unto others that which you would not have them do unto you* is a venerable guideline as to how each individual should behave toward any other individual. The practice of mutuality and reciprocity is perhaps as close as any of us can come to the attainment of justice.

• Or test what is good and just by applying *the principle of universality* to one's maxims. A sample maxim: I have a moral right to my life, livelihood, liberty. Is this just? Yes, if one can concede a similar right to every other individual. I can! Try it in reverse: I have a moral right to take the life, livelihood, liberty of another. Just? Only if I can rationally concede the right of murder, theft, enslavement to everyone else. I cannot concede this right to anyone; thus, it is neither good nor just.[2]

• The institution of freedom, if properly defined, suffices to render justice to each individual. John Stuart Mill said:

> The only freedom which deserves the name, is that of *pursuing our own good in our own way, so long as we do not attempt to deprive others of theirs,* or impede their efforts to obtain it.

• My own definition of freedom, if practiced, would assure universal justice: *No man-concocted restraints against the release of creative energy.* This is to say that no one would inhibit any individual in any way whatsoever except to curb his destructive actions: fraud, violence, misrepresentation, predation, and the like.

The formulas above are four ways of expressing substantially the same thought: justice—in contrast to a grant of privilege—is the absence of any deterrent to the creative aspirations of any individual. Let each person pursue his own ends so long as he does not impede the peaceful objectives of other individuals. Justice, when rightly defined, is "the cement of society," as Alexander Hamilton phrased it.

---

[2]Immanuel Kant, *The Foundations of the Metaphysics of Morals,* New York, 1959.

We now come to what is euphemistically referred to as social justice, though it is in theory and practice the very opposite of justice. Social justice reflects the mood of our times. It is of ancient origin, to be sure, though still in use as a device that politicians and social planners find convenient to gain votes and power. Social justice has no case except the lust for position; it has no rational content and simply manifests the little-god syndrome.

IGNORING THE INDIVIDUAL

In the practice of so-called social justice, the individual is ignored, absolutely! Instead, the population and the economy are dealt with in enormous lumps: individuals are vaguely classified into the haves and the have-nots, treated as voting blocs of farmers, wage earners, old folks, oppressed minorities, disaster victims, slum dwellers, and countless other legions in "the war on poverty."

Social justice is the game of "robbing selected Peter to pay for collective Paul." This form of political behavior seeks the gain of some at the expense of others, and cannot be distinguished from Marx's "from each according to ability, to each according to need." The fact that social justice parallels a thought of Marx is not what condemns it; rather, it is the thwarting of justice that begs our censure. Test social justice under the preceding formulas of justice to perceive the difference.

• *The Golden Rule:* If you would not condone others coercively taking from you to feather their nests you could not, perforce, take from them to feather your own. Social justice is at odds with this rule.

● *Universality:* If you cannot rationally approve the practice of legal plunder by everyone as a means of prospering, you cannot agree to it as a means of personal emolument. Social justice is wholly antagonistic to this principle.

● *Pursuing one's own good so long as others are not deprived of theirs:* Social justice involves precisely the opposite procedure—depriving others to gain one's ends.

● *No man-concocted restraints against the release of creative energy:* Social justice promises to reward the idle by punishing and restraining those who have exercised creative energy.

So-called social justice is man's greatest injustice to man, antisocial in every respect; not the cement of society, but the lust for power and privilege and the seed of man's corruption and downfall.

Finally, social justice in no way fits the claim of its advocates: an expression of mercy and pity. These virtues are strictly personal attributes and are expressed only in the voluntary giving of one's own, never in the seizure and redistribution of someone else's possessions.

Morally and ethically motivated citizens can condone a philosophy of so-called social justice only if they fail to see its terrible injustice.

15

THE WINDS THAT BLOW

Men, it has been well said, think in herds; it will be seen that they go mad in herds, while they only re-cover their senses slowly, and one by one.

—CHARLES MACKAY

There are literally millions of people in the United States and in other countries—even in Russia—who are greatly distressed by the rising tides of unreason; old and popular delusions are overpowering some of the noblest truths mankind has ever come upon. Civilizations are in decline. Now, what is the customary way of coping with this devolutionary trend? With but few exceptions the distraught millions attempt to remedy the madness by counterattacks; they try to "straighten out" the rascals; they try to outvote and outtalk them; they call them unkind names; in a word, they go to war with them! Tactically, all of this is utterly futile, harmful rather than helpful, and a waste of time, energy, and money. Or, so I believe!

Put it this way: Winds of nonsensical opinion, of emotion and nonreason, appear to be as much beyond our control as are the atmospheric winds. Further, we are about as fallible in assigning causes to one as to the other. In either case, we appear to be helpless, victims of the winds that blow. No one knows the causes of the socialistic nonsense sweeping over the world and, thus, we are, for the most part, unaware of how to replace socialism with the freedom way of life. After forty years of effort, featured by trial and a great deal of error, I am convinced that it is futile to attempt to reform those who voice and lend credence to these winds of socialism. Does this mean that we are totally helpless, or is there a course of action that holds promise?

Reflect on atmospheric winds. They range all the way from gentle breezes to violent hurricanes, coming first from this direction and then that, blowing hot or mild or freezing. What causes these fantastic variations? The meteorologists, who have my respect, confess that they do not know all the answers. Yes, tiltings of the earth account for changes, as does the distribution of land and water. Mountain slopes play a part and, perhaps, ocean currents do also. But what causes these causes? Even if we knew, man could not alter them. They are, we might say, the ultimate given; and we live with these winds—like it or not.

PRESSURE BELTS

While all analogies are dangerous devices for reasoning, there is one aspect of meteorological knowledge that suggests for us a course of action. It is this: "The prevailing wind systems of the earth blow from the several belts of high pressure toward adjacent low pressure belts."

Low pressure belts are featured by fog and smog, poor visibility—the kind of weather usually described as disagreeable. Winds come sweeping into these areas as water rushes with great velocity over Niagara Falls. Winds and waters obeying their nature, speed up as there are depressions. Low pressure areas are among the known causes of atmospheric winds.

Analogous to low pressure areas are individuals of little understanding. The nonsense in the minds of men, omnipresent among us if often somewhat dormant, is activated, whipped into a fury, as it rushes into mentalities too empty or depressed to care about the difference between slavery and freedom. Indeed, one can guess how limited the understanding by observing the ferocity of the winds of nonsensical opinion. We can only gauge that in today's world understanding is woefully deficient!

What does this suggest as the only way to correct the devolutionary trend? The sole answer is to be found in a personal response. You are the answer! And so am I!

Assume a goodly number of individuals so well grounded in the freedom philosophy that socialistic notions, regardless of how cleverly phrased, can make no impact—none whatsoever. The winds of nonsensical opinion would cease to blow. There simply would be no low pressure troughs to set them in motion, no empty heads into which they might flow. Checkmate!

There we have it: the perfection of self-understanding as against reforming others—the former possible, the latter futile. Why futile? Bad ideas cannot be made more sensible by combatting those who voice them. We need but recognize that ideas, good or bad, seize hold of the individual; it is not the other way around. I do not possess an idea; it possesses me. "As a man thinketh in his heart, so is he."

The freedom devotee who attempts to set the rascals straight, by whatever device, poses as a magician or miracle worker. He assumes that he can do to others that which he cannot or will not do to himself. No one can concentrate on the perfection of his own thinking when fretting about the deficiency of others. By pursuing the impossible, he neglects the only remedy—the one that is within reach.

The one that is within reach! Nearly all of us who favor freedom assume mistakenly that we have nothing more to reach for, that merely being against socialism suffices. The fact? There is not one among us who has more than scratched the surface toward his own upgrading. There is a fair way to test this assertion: merely observe how few, if any, seek our light, anxious for an audience with us. Ours is a problem of reaching, now and forever, not for others to reform, but for truths that might attract others.

ONE AT A TIME

Reflection makes it plain that this one-by-one emergence from socialism through self-improvement is the way it should be. Man's purpose is to grow in awareness, perception, consciousness. It is not my earthly role to make carbon copies of me. Nor is this the role of any other person. Any attempt to cast others in your or my image is, of itself, a denial of the freedom philosophy. Reformers are not on my side and, hopefully, not on yours.

Another view of the wind analogy: In the heat of emotion or battle, individuals tend to create low pressure areas. Other ideas then flow in to displace such hot air, not always or necessarily more truthful concepts, but at least more welcome in a given environment. If one does not like the prevailing winds, the best he can do is to refine and polish and render more understandable and acceptable his own views, thus removing himself as a source of hot air and disturbance.

To tell the truth may be disturbing; but only because it is not told with sufficient skill and patience. The same may be said of a falsehood. But Nature, I believe, is on the side of truth, and will reveal her secrets to anyone who searches diligently and well.

I know the rebuttal: the sole way is the slow way. Granted! Yet, slow as it may be, it is the fastest way there is. Speeding in the wrong direction is to lose, not gain, headway. Anyone who potentially can have a helpful hand in this matter of the winds that blow can easily improve himself if he puts his mind to it.

Imagine a goodly number well versed in the freedom philosophy, impervious to socialistic nonsense. Here we would have a new and greatly needed high pressure area from which would come only gentle breezes—warm and soft-spoken as the answer of one whose counsel has been sought.

16

TO THINE OWN SELF
BE TRUE

*I cannot find language of sufficient
energy to convey my sense of the
sacredness of private integrity.*

—EMERSON

Ralph Waldo Emerson, one of the strongest minds and most energetic phrasers of ideas, acknowledges a weakness: an inability to explain the exalted role of integrity in the life of man. In this respect, I find myself with a conviction identical to his, and a similar inability, no less distressing. At least, I am in good company.

Integrity is rarely mentioned or included among the virtues. The so-called cardinal virtues, as advanced in theology, are prudence, justice, fortitude, temperance. Integrity is omitted. I found, upon checking the largest of all quotation books, that integrity does not appear among the more than 1,000 headings.[1] Indeed, so much neglected is this virtue, that

---

[1] *The Home Book of Proverbs, Maxims and Familiar Phrases,* selected and arranged by Burton Stevenson, New York, 1948.

one is tempted to side with Bernard Dougall: "Integrity was a word he couldn't even spell, let alone define." Such is the unawareness of its meaning and importance!

When it comes to listing the virtues, I know only those that are important to me. Integrity is by all means first and foremost. For the others—charity,[2] intelligence,[3] justice,[4] love,[5] and humility—I have no precise ranking. To me they are tied for second place.

At the outset, it may be helpful to draw the distinction between integrity and wisdom, for my definitions so closely parallel each other.

> Integrity is an accurate reflection in word and deed of whatever one's highest *conscience* dictates as right.
> Wisdom is whatever one's highest *consciousness* perceives as truth.

Conceded, one's highest conscience may not in fact be right but it is as close to righteousness as one can get. Also, one's highest consciousness may not be truth but as nearly approximates wisdom as is within one's reach. Fallibility applies in either case!

People differ in their evaluation of Emerson's philosophy, but all concede that his proclaimed positions, written and oral, were accurate reflections of whatever his highest con-

---

[2]Lloyd Douglas, *Magnificent Obsession,* New York, 1969.

[3]John Erskine, *Moral Obligations to be Intelligent & Other Essays,* Freeport, New York, 1921.

[4]See preceding chapter, "Justice versus Social Justice."

[5]For an explanation that love is light, see my *Then Truth Will Out, op. cit.,* pp. 11-20.

science dictated as righteous. Never, to our knowledge, did he bend to expediency, that is, resort to deviations from conscience to gain favor or popularity with others. So rigorous were his spiritual convictions that he was at odds with the numerous religious orthodoxies and took no pains to conceal his innermost sentiments.[6] Attuned to his conscience, he stood ramrod straight. As this rare posture is sometimes phrased, he sought approval from God, not men. Integrity!

Yet, Emerson, conscious of the sacredness of integrity, could find no words energetic enough to convey his sense of its importance. In the light of his genius as a thinker and a phraser of ideas, why his confessed inability to handle this concept? Why could he not explain the meaning of integrity to others?

THE SACREDNESS OF INTEGRITY

As I see it, the answer lies in one of his own words: the *sacredness* of integrity. This virtue is in a moral and spiritual realm so far above normal experience that we possess no words to portray its meaning. It borders on the Infinite and, thus, is beyond our working vocabulary. This explains why it is so seldom included among the virtues. For these reasons, I am convinced that integrity cannot be taught; at best, it can only be caught. And, then, only by those who devoutly wish to be so graced!

Such integrity as I possess was caught, not taught. Fortunately, I came upon a high-ranking business executive, Wil-

---

[6]For an excellent selection of Emerson's thoughts, see *The Gospel of Emerson* by Newton Dillaway, *op. cit.*

liam C. Mullendore, Southern California Edison Company, who was no less an exemplar of this virtue than Emerson. Never in the many years of our intimate acquaintance have I observed him giving ground to expediency—conscience always in the driver's seat! The question is, why did his exemplarity impress itself more upon me than upon others who also knew him well? Perhaps this cannot be answered. True, this unusual trait in him excited my admiration. But why me, of all his friends? Who knows!

Here is a possible explanation. Having had but little formal schooling, and always conscious of not knowing much, I resolved, some forty-five years ago, to associate myself with individuals from whom I might learn—superior persons. Parenthetically, these are not difficult to find and almost without exception are pleased to be so regarded. In any event, I was aware of an enormous unknown and, at the same time, eager to learn. In this state of mind one goes in search of that which is generally not known. Does such openness, perhaps, account for my coming upon this remarkable man and his integrity? All that I can specifically identify is a state of mind best described as wanting-to-know-it-ness. Would extensive formal schooling have lessened this? Again, who knows! The fortunate chain of events is shrouded in mysterious forces I do not understand.

THE LAW OF RIGHTEOUSNESS

Mysterious indeed is the way of life of anyone guided by integrity. There comes to mind a recent day at the office. Whether in conversations across the desk, or over the phone, or in replies to letters, the answers were invariably "No!" Why? Every proposal was at odds with what I believed to be right, that is, contrary to the dictates of conscience. Thank heaven, that day was exceptional; happily, many questions can be answered "Yes." Nonetheless, integrity must rule the word, the deed, the action. This is the law of righteousness.

The temptation—sometimes close to overwhelming—is to gain the approval of some prestigious individual by saying "Yes" when a "No" is right. In resisting this temptation, what is required? We must learn how to say "No" without giving offense, in a word, rise above cantankerousness. This art, if achieved, is highly rewarding, one that upgrades the intellect and the soul. It has its genesis in the practice of integrity.

Unless integrity is weighed and found worthy, the common conviction is that its practice would leave one a loner, an "odd ball" whose actions would drive friends away. The very opposite is the case; integrity has a magnetic effect; it attracts others. Why? The practitioners of this virtue can be trusted, and trust has drawing power, as daily experiences attest.

NOT DANGEROUS TO BE HONEST

Years ago, when the attractiveness of adhering strictly to conscience was more of a new idea to me, I was invited to spend an evening with a dozen of the country's leading businessmen. The subject for discussion had to do with the so-called Full Employment Act, then before the Congress. Most of the talk favored the tactic of opposing the measure by subterfuge, dealing under the table, so to speak—repulsive to me. When finally asked for my view, I hesitated a moment. To tell them exactly what I thought would do me in, damage my career, or so I imagined. But, I told them! Never have I had a more rewarding experience. From that day forward those twelve were devoted friends, inviting me to counsel time after time. Why? Integrity!

An aside: While it is not dangerous to be honest, this does not mean that one must necessarily divulge all of his innermost thoughts. Many doubtless deserve further incubation. But once a position is taken and expressed, let there be in it no deviation from conscience.

Imagine that a fair percentage of citizens of this nation were practicing what their highest conscience dictates as right. No man could ever be elevated to public office except as he exemplifies integrity. Think what a change this would make in the national scene. Only statesmen; never a charlatan!

WHO IS EDUCABLE?

And who among us is truly educable in the higher realms of thought? Only people of integrity! The person who pays no heed to conscience is forever the victim of expediencies; he is governed by fickle opinions, pressures, mass sentiments, a desire for momentary acclaim. Wisdom—whatever one's highest consciousness perceives as truth—is out of range simply because integrity—whatever one's highest conscience dictates as right—is not observed.

As if the above were not reason enough to strive for integrity! However, by far the most important reason remains: its *sacredness.* Though new to me, I now discover that this idea was perceived nearly 2,000 years ago:

> The light of the body is the eye: if therefore thine eye be single, thy whole body shall be full of light.—Matthew 6:22

In other words, the light of the body is truth, wisdom, enlightenment. The eye is perception. And what is the meaning of "if thine eye be single"? Refer to Webster for the definition of "single" as here used: "Not deceitful or artful, simple, honest, sincere." Shakespeare used the word in this same sense: "I speak with a *single* heart."

SINGLENESS OF PURPOSE

Single, in this sense, is directly linked with *integer,* meaning "Whole, entire, not divided." Contrasted to *single* is *double,* which has the same original root as the word "duplicity." Such phrases as "double-dealing," and "double-talk" convey this connotation. *Integrity* is related to *integer;* and *single* as used here, refers to *integrity.*

Phrased in modern idiom, Matthew's insight would read as follows:

> Enlightenment of the intellect and spirit of man depends on his powers of perception. If these powers be free from duplicity, that is, if they be grounded in pure integrity, man will be as much graced with enlightenment—wisdom—as is within his capability.

Whatever the mysterious Universal Power—the radiant energy that flows through all life—it is blocked, cut off, stifled by duplicity in any of its forms. Expediency, lying, double talk, and the like are ferments of the soul through which Universal Power does not and cannot flow. "A double-minded man is unstable in all his ways."[7]

Only in integrity—when the "eye be single" —do the powers of perception grow, evolve, emerge, hatch. Then the "whole body shall be full of light." Then, and only then, are such virtues as charity, intelligence, justice, love, humility within our reach.

Finally, if we believe that we should not do unto others that which we would not have them do unto us—a concern for others as well as self—we have one more among all the compelling reasons why we should strive first and foremost for integrity. Shakespeare put it well:

> To thine own self be true,
> And it must follow, as the night the day,
> Thou canst not then be false to any man.

---

[7]James 1:8.

17

THE ROLE OF
EXUBERANCE

*If you do not expect the unex-
pected, you will not find it.*
—HERACLITUS

The trend is away from liberty; the problem is how to reverse
direction. How shall we go about this task? Do we need to
rouse the masses? No, ours is not a numbers problem. There
are tens of thousands, perhaps millions of persons—more than
the job requires—who frown on all forms of authoritarian collectivism and who favor liberty. The failure of this multitude
to generate a trend toward liberty lies in inept methods; indeed, most of us, by our lack of proper posture, aggravate
rather than alleviate our social woes. Unwittingly, the would-
be friends of liberty aid its foes.

If this point be granted, an inference is plain: the correct
methods we are neglecting must be composed of generally
unsuspected attitudes and techniques or else we would now
be employing them. If they were obvious, someone would be
practicing them ere this. Thus, if the customary tactics are not

working, perhaps we ought to turn our expectations toward the unexpected.

A wise person taught me a valuable lesson years ago: whenever any course of action is not joyous, it has error at its heart. Here is a guideline as to when one is off course; it tells when to say "no" to self, a valuable negative! However, the full potentialities of joyousness have just dawned upon me. For this insight, I am indebted to "Toward An Exuberant Europe," a chapter in a recent and remarkable book by Robert McClintock.[1]

To examine the role of exuberance, good humor, joyousness, congeniality, or just plain fun in society requires first of all that we have some idea as to what is meant by society.

WHAT IS SOCIETY?

Ortega wrote, "We know society is comprised of *I's* and *You's* but beyond this we have not the remotest idea of what society is." As I see it, society is any number of *I's* and *You's* —a few or many—who socialize or are in some state of intercourse with each other, or, as Georg Simmel put it, "wherever several individuals enter into reciprocal relations . . . the same form and the same kind of socialization can arise in connection with the most varied elements and take place for the most diverse ends. Socialization in general takes place as well in a religious congregation as in a band of conspirators, in a trust as well as in a school of art, in a public gathering as in a

---

[1]Robert McClintock, *Man and His Circumstances: Ortega as Educator,* New York, 1971.

family." Thus, in this sense, a society may be a tribe, clan, mob, alumni reunion, or the American People.

To test the thesis here at issue, let us see how it might work out on a small scale. Imagine a thousand persons so distraught by authoritarianism in their respective countries that they decide not to face and help solve local problems but resolve instead to establish a Shangri-La of their own. So, they acquire a far-off island and incorporate a new Republic. Here, they believe, men may make a fresh start! What are their chances for building the good society? Upon what does a realization of their hopes depend?

The success or failure of an enterprise such as this would rest entirely upon the quality of their dispositions: moral, spiritual, intellectual, tolerative. Even if someone wrote a Constitution for these migrants superior to our original, it would not make one whit of difference. The outcome of this experiment would depend on how well these people get along with each other, the level at which they socialize. This, in turn, is determined by what kinds of persons they are. Make the bleak assumption that most of them are know-it-alls, quick to anger with everyone who does not agree. The prospect of realizing their ambitions for an ideal community are nil in an atmosphere of disrespect, antagonism, dissent. As Erasmus observed, "Where there is hatred in judgment, judgment is blind." Like begets like! Rules and disciplines originating in active intolerance cannot help but spread discontent. People not of a genial mien would be well advised to stay home!

On the other hand, were these people to master an opposite posture, that is, were they of the kind that could have fun or find joy in striving for their ideals, an improved society would be a viable prospect. Why? As Ortega suggests, creation is born in exuberance. This is to say, creation is never the child of anger. So, let us try to apply this finding, this principle, to our own situation.

THE JOYOUS APPROACH

As a starter, take stock of all the antisocialist, profreedom individuals of your acquaintance. How many can you find who are not angry—who are not name-callers? True, some express their spite in elegant prose; but spite is spite regardless of the verbal dress it wears. Do you not find that the vast majority are out of temper? Embittered warriors? Intolerance, confrontation, disgust with those of opposed views engender not improvement in others but resentment, not progress but regress. This, I insist, is a mood that does more harm than good; dead silence would be preferable. "When men sink into despair, they cannot give birth to a new age; they can only stand mute, watching and waiting."[2] What is the remedy? Exuberance!

Our hope for an improved society, as with everything creative, requires a happy breed of aspiring idealists—exuberant individuals. Where are these to be found? Among the very devotees of freedom who are presently angry! How is this switch in posture to be brought about? By simply trying it, and proving its efficacy! Rejecting what does not work and

---

[2]This and all subsequent quotations are from Ortega or his biographer, McClintock.

embracing that which does! This is merely a matter of knowing what is and is not practical.

Put it another way: *Our problem is not getting into the fight but into the play!* I have learned over the years, not merely to tolerate but to enjoy the weather—rain when I wish to golf and sunshine when the garden needs water, and so on. Why, then, can I not become more tolerant of the error I behold in others? Unless this be accomplished, I can never get into the play. Exuberance, on which all creative actions depend, is out of the question.

SELF-TRANSCENDENCE

Self-transcendence is the requirement. "Now they can do nothing more with themselves unless they transcend themselves." What is the meaning of this? It simply means to rise above oneself, that is, to engage in thought and discussion over and beyond the daily grind of, shall we say, making a living. "The free man exercises his freedom by *creating* duties for himself. . . . Moral perfection, like all perfection, is a *sportive quality, something that one adds luxuriously to what is necessary and indispensable."* (Italics added)

The phrase, sportive quality, lends clarity to this theme. Sport, in the minds of many, has come to mean spectacles such as those witnessed at the Roman Colosseum where Christians were thrown to the lions, or in Spain where a matador slays the bull, or in this country where millions flock to prize fights, professional football, baseball, and the like. The sportive quality Ortega commends is not that of a spectator; it refers to the spirit with which we enter into extracurricular activities over and beyond necessity—a personal game, drawing on untapped faculties. Analogous examples: climbers planning how to scale the Matterhorn. Or me and you figuring out how to write and read this idea in clarity. Such games are played in exuberance; they fall in the realm of just plain fun—*serious but sportive!*

In the area of our concern—an improving society—we need only remind ourselves that the rules by which we live are not, in the final analysis, governed by constitutions and other legal gadgetry. Argentina, for example, copied and then improved the U.S.A. model, but to no avail. Economic, social, and political chaos reigns there now and for the simple reason that the general thinking, the overall moral standards, ethical concepts, and respect for others—reciprocal relations—were inferior to the formal document. Might as well tack a sign, "This is Heaven," on a den of dictators!

ALL CREATIVE WORKS

"As Ortega saw it, all of man's great cultural works—law, science, religion, morality, art—were originated in sporting acts." Once reflected upon, it is clear that all advance—every creative result—has to have this origin. For it is only when men are freely thinking and happily discoursing about ideals that they discover any of the rules for better living. Why? It is because these are the rules for self-improvement, and they arise out of self-improvement. They are believed by us because they grow out of ourselves—and we abide by such rules.

During the final session of a recent FEE Seminar, the participants were laughing and having a high old time, as happy a mood as I have ever experienced. Consider this joviality in the light of the very serious and idealistic subject matter with which they had been wrestling for two days. I interrupted the exuberance of this rare occasion—having fun while thinking—to make a point: Please take note of how joyous we are. This means that we are on the right track.

Were each of us to acquire this posture in his respective orbit, we would soon appreciate the role of exuberance in society, for it is the only mood and spirit that can turn the trend toward liberty. Try it!

18

YE OF LITTLE FAITH

Despotism may govern without faith, but Liberty cannot.

—TOCQUEVILLE

This is a moment in history when despotism is rampant the world over. Misrule has reached its apogee in nation after nation as men fight for position in the despotic darkness. If the U.S.A. lags somewhat in this fall from societal grace, time affords scant comfort to a body falling out of control.

Despotism has numerous labels which most of us frown upon: communism, socialism, Nazism, fascism, Fabianism. So, on the home front, the politicians and social planners devise new labels with favorable connotations: "New Deal," "New Republicanism," and the like. But, regardless of the window dressing, despotism is, quite simply, some persons lording it over other persons. Thus, whatever the political theology be called, if one would assess the degree of despotism, then let him forget the labels and, instead, estimate how much coercive control is being exercised by some over others. This is the measuring rod.

Liberty—despotism's opposite—can be defined as no man-concocted restraints against the release of creative human energy.

Now to the point of this inquiry. Tocqueville suggests that despotism may govern without faith, but liberty cannot. I wish to examine this claim. If false, we can forget the subject of faith so far as political economy is concerned; if true, we have some serious work cut out for ourselves.

DESPOTIC RULE

Can a despot govern others? All history attests to the fact that people by the billions have been so governed; they have been subjected to the will of authoritarians. Persons backed by a constabulary—coercive force—can, with few exceptions, compel others to do their bidding. As to this type of governance, there appears to be no question. This, despotic rule can do!

Is faith required to effect such governance? None whatsoever, unless the meaning of faith be grossly corrupted. Using the term in its correct sense, merely observe that faith guides neither the majority of those so governed nor those who despotically govern.

As to those governed: The despotism here at issue is a consensual power, that is, it can exist only with a consenting majority. Wherever and whenever this arrangement prevails, we can conclude that it is more agreeable than not, that most of the people want a shepherd and sheep dogs. They prefer having their lives run and guided for them. To be one's own man is not sufficiently attractive and, thus, they acquiesce in the herding. They comply passively—without real conviction or faith.

As to those who govern: Here we need only recognize the innate variability of human beings. Except in one generally overlooked respect, each of us differs from all others. Indeed, aside from this one exception, each of us varies from one moment to the next; not for one second does any one of us ever stay put! In what manner, then, are we identical? *In our inability to control the life of another beneficially.* In this respect, we are all alike in the sense that zeros are identical. To get it into my head that I can run or control your life better than you is nothing less than egomania. This affliction cannot, by the wildest stretch of the imagination, be called a faith; it is a psychosis. Despotism can indeed govern without faith. Score one for Tocqueville!

TOCQUEVILLE ON AMERICA

Now to the claim that liberty cannot govern without faith. Anyone familiar with the thinking and observations set forth by Tocqueville in his monumental work, *Democracy In America,* realizes that, when referring to liberty, he had no reference to "govern" in its over-riding sense. He meant only that individual liberty could not preside as a way of life among a people without widespread personal faith. And as to faith, he meant a spiritual faith. The sense of his thinking is to be found in the following:

I sought for the greatness and genius of America in fertile fields and boundless forests; it was not there. I sought for it in her free schools and her institutions of learning; it was not there. I sought for it in her matchless Constitution and democratic congress; it was not there. Not until I went to the churches of America and found them aflame with righteousness did I understand the greatness and genius of America. America is great because America is good. When America ceases to be good, America will cease to be great.[1]

To introduce this phase of my inquiry, let me quote a friend's question: "I do not have to believe in God to believe in freedom, do I?" My reply: "No, you do not, but if all citizens were atheists there would be no freedom." While this conviction of mine is beyond "proof" in any scientific sense, the evidence for it is abundant.[2]

Conceded, there are many so-called or self-styled atheists— people confessing to no spiritual faith—whose lives are exemplary insofar as societal relationships are concerned and who, at the same time, are not afflicted with egomania. But these persons have a strange and fortunate immunity. Those who are unable to concede the reality of something above and beyond the individual expose themselves to a grave danger: the belief that there is nothing beyond their own finite minds. Such potential despots exist by the millions, from dullards to the relatively brilliant, and are easily identified—always theirs is "the last word."

Let us also concede that in today's world there are other millions who proclaim a spiritual faith—including many

---

[1]This quotation is found on pages 12-13 of the once popular school text by F. A. Magruder, *American Government: A Textbook on the Problems of Democracy.* Except for the last two sentences, this is Magruder's paraphrase of Tocqueville's words.

[2]For my explanation, see *Deeper Than You Think,* Irvington, N.Y., 1967, pp. 15-27.

clergymen—who are as much afflicted with egomania as are any avowed atheists. Such men are deficient in the awe which a proper sense of God's majesty induces; for, in my view, it is unlikely that anyone with a deep and abiding faith in an Infinite Consciousness can be other than joyously humble— free from the little-god Syndrome.[3] Attempting to run the lives of others is unthinkable, once this spiritual belief nourishes the roots of one's reflections. But, be this as it may, it is admittedly difficult to draw a sharp line between affectation or superstition on the one hand and genuine spiritual faith on the other. Degrees and depths of faith cannot be measured by our customary yardsticks.

FAITH AND LIBERTY

Along the lines of these observations, it seems that the presence or absence of spiritual faith—as an external observer might measure it—does not in itself assure or deny either despotism or liberty. Millions of people have been slaughtered in the name of "religion."[4] Also, liberty has been ascribed to God as its Author. What, then, is the relevance of faith to liberty?

Spiritual faith provides the foundation without which liberty is impossible. Bear in mind, however, that monstrosities as well as noble edifices can be erected on sound foundations. This is to say that despotism as well as liberty can arise from

---

[3]"No man can believe in his own omnipotence who has any sense of God's power."—Edmund A. Opitz in *The Freeman,* April 1971, p. 198.

[4]See *Grey Eminence* by Aldous Huxley, New York, 1941.

spiritual faith. History has many examples of the former; the America that Tocqueville studied was an example of the latter.

Suppose atheism were all-pervading—nothing recognized or conceived of as above the finite minds of imperfect men. In this situation, there would be no fundamental point of reference beyond the little minds, all at sixes and sevens. A centrifugal force would dominate: millions, each with "the last word," spinning apart—every which way—with their assorted and arbitrary notions. Here is the excuse for despotism to come "to the rescue"—one of the little minds "riding herd," as we say.

Shift now to a people "aflame with righteousness," possessing a deep spiritual faith, that is, aware of an Infinite Consciousness or Intelligence or Light to which each is related, at best, as an image or infinitesimal manifestation. Here is Omniscience before which each stands in awe and from which he attempts to draw enlightenment! Thus altered from atheism to faith, there is a centripetal instead of a centrifugal force in play. The tendency is now to cohesion, not toward identity, for there is a directional ingathering toward enlightenment and a tolerance for our fantastic creative variations, whatever turn they might take. Each his own man! Catholicity! The push would be in this direction—toward righteousness.

A SOLID FOUNDATION

This splendid faith, however, provides no more than the sound foundation. Both despotism and liberty have been structured on it. Faith, we must remember, has to do with the individual's relationship to or conception of his Maker. It does not, of itself, extend beyond this.

Despotism and liberty, on the other hand, have to do with social relationships—the way man relates to other men. Faith does not suffice for the building of society; it provides only the necessary foundation. For an improvement in the societal situation there must be added to faith another quality of which man is capable: *reason.*

Let us observe how our Founding Fathers combined faith and reason to structure the nearest approximation to human liberty ever attained:

> . . . that all men *are endowed by their Creator* with certain unalienable Rights, that among these are Life, Liberty and the pursuit of Happiness.

How does this proposition qualify as *reason* added to the faith that was then so dominant? Simple: With their faith as the foundation, the authors of the Declaration took the rational step of seating the Creator as the single point of reference, thereby making all men precisely as equal before the civil law as all men are equal before the Creator. They pronounced the Creator as sovereign and, by so doing, implicitly denied the sovereignty of any combination of seekers after power—organized as government or otherwise. Liberty and justice for all!

The fact that the foundation (faith) appears to be crumbling and that reason appears to be taking flight, in no way lessens the truth of Tocqueville's observation that liberty cannot exist without faith. And I would add: or without *reason.*

Our hope—the heartening possibility—is that these appearances are utterly false, as appearances often are. For all you or I know, both faith and reason of a quality never before known may, at this very moment, be gestating in the souls and minds of men on the grand scale. We believe in liberty. So, why not believe in what is required of men to achieve this way of life? There is magic in believing. Why? Because, as Bulwer-Lytton phrased it, "In belief lies the secret of all valuable exertion."

19

THE MYSTIQUE OF WISDOM

The wise man endeavors to shine in
himself; the fool to outshine others.
—ADDISON

Suppose I were observed trying to impart my "wisdom" to a corpse. The verdict would be, "Read's off his rocker." But I am convinced that it is equally unrealistic of me to try to ram my wisdom in to the head of anybody, living or dead. If I tried this on a corpse, I would be making a fool of myself; in the case of the living, most people today, based on their own actions, would think of me as a sensible worker in freedom's vineyard. Yet, in either case, I would be acting wastefully, foolishly.

Wisdom! What is it and who has it? Socrates remarked, "The Delphic oracle said I was the wisest of all the Greeks. It is because that I alone, of all the Greeks, know that I know nothing." Only in comparison to the rest of us was Socrates wise; compared to the infinite unknown, he knew nothing. He was aware of his own fallibility, and suspected that no one knows anything *for certain.*

Any discussion of wisdom, to be useful in day-to-day life, must be confined to the infinitesimal bits each possesses. No human being, past or present, regardless of how exalted his opinion of himself, can be rated any higher than Socrates— a know-nothing. All of us, without exception, are in this category.

Having relegated myself, as well as all others, to the smallness that befits our attainments—our place in the Cosmic Order—how are we to define wisdom? How explain its mysteries? How be realistic? An observation by Lactantius in the 4th Century A.D. is pertinent: *"The first point of wisdom is to discern that which is false; the second, to know that which is true."*

While it is possible to detect errors and expose inconsistencies in a set of ideas, the falsity of a doctrine is not really grasped until the true position is worked out. No one understands the falseness of socialism until he is familiar with the case for freedom. Using the axiom of Lactantius, we may conclude that one's wisdom is limited to the truth perceived.

WHAT IS TRUTH?

In short, to evaluate wisdom and its mysteries, it is necessary that we examine truth. What is truth? *It is only that which one's highest consciousness dictates as right.* This may not in fact be truth but is as close as any person can possibly come to it. The idea that the earth is flat was at one time accepted as true by millions of people; now millions of people hold that the earth is a sphere. That the sun revolves around the earth was a truth to Ptolemy and his contemporaries.

Copernicus, Galileo and others became conscious of a contrary view. This change in perception has been going on in every field of endeavor—in all disciplines—since the dawn of consciousness. And the end is not likely.

The record suggests that we should be cautious about certainty on any matter. This is but another way of admitting that one's finite consciousness falls indescribably short of Infinite Consciousness. Yet, to live life at its best, we must heed whatever our highest consciousness dictates as right. Not to do so is to bury ourselves in more error—more falsehood—than is necessary. This is the height of foolishness.

At my level of consciousness, there are numerous bits of seeming wisdom—truths to me. The most profound, the one about which I am most certain, is: "Seek ye first the Kingdom of God and his Righteousness, and these things shall be added unto you." This simply means to seek, first and foremost, truth and righteousness. This is the way and the only way to contact all of the wisdom that is within one's reach. This is *the* key to such potentialities as one possesses. Or, so it seems to me.

THE NEED TO SEEK

For the sake of the point I wish to make, concede that this Biblical counsel is a truth: wisdom. There it is on the printed page, first in Aramaic, then in Greek, Latin, English, and other languages. *Merely note that the sentence has no initiatory powers whatsoever!* It does not, it cannot, propel or insinuate itself into a single consciousness. As light, it can be seen; as light, it cannot see.

Who may see? Exclusively, the seekers! "Seek ye first" has more meaning than first meets the eye. Were this wisdom only in Aramaic, or Greek, or Latin, I would not see it without first mastering the language in which it appears. Even then, while I may read the words, it does not follow that I really apprehend this wisdom. In addition to seeking the words, I must seek the meaning. The initiative is all mine. Thus, I may see and apprehend a bit of wisdom if I am capable of taking it unto myself; that wisdom is utterly powerless to fasten itself onto me. Herein lies one of the mysteries.

Now for the shocker, a view that is contrary to reform movements, past and present. *A bit of wisdom in your head or mine is precisely as powerless to advance itself as is that same wisdom in a printed page.* It is there to be taken if there be any takers—seekers. Your wisdom or mine, such as it is, may be drawn on by another if he so chooses; it cannot be injected into the consciousness of another for the simple reason that each person is in charge of his own doors of perception. Trying to inject "wisdom" into the mind of a living person is precisely as fruitless as trying to inject wisdom into a corpse. Is this a truth? If not, I am disappointed. If you or I could do this to others, then others could do it to us. Heaven forbid!

The challenge that makes sense is to become a seeker—to aim at self-enlightenment. I should not only refrain from trying to pump my wisdom into others but should rid myself of any such ambition, cast it from my mind entirely. Fretting about how ignorant others are and attempting to set them straight is to parry with shadows. One cannot take the high road of improving self while tilting at windmills.

Another mystery comes to mind: the transmission of wisdom is not hindered by time or space, provided we maintain an open mind to what may be seen!

THE LIGHT OF SOCRATES

Socrates who lived 2,400 years before me and who worked 5,300 miles from where I do has, I am certain, given me more light than he gave his wife, Xanthippe, who shared his abode. Proximity in time and space does not necessarily have anything to do with how much light one gleans from another. All of our experiences, if carefully examined, attest to this.

Indeed, intimacy often throws up a barrier to deter one person drawing on the lights of another. Socrates, while brilliant of mind, was slovenly of person, or so it is reported. Sloppiness around the house could easily be the criterion by which a wife would judge a husband in all respects. Relegate an individual to an unfavorable status for whatever reason and he is likely to remain in that status regardless of any qualities he might possess. The sight of another's faults tends to blind us to his virtues. Blinded by seeing, of all things!

Assuming that Socrates was slovenly, that trait makes no impression on me for I am not a witness of it—only of his illuminations; they alone have mirrored their way through the centuries to me. But I note a deplorable tendency on my part to seek no light whatsoever from those whose appearance disgusts me or whose ideological or philosophical positions I regard as "cracked." My inclination is to relegate them to the scrap heap without even looking for some enlightening thought they might possess. This brings up an embarrassing question: are they alone in being off course? Perhaps I am on a wrong tack!

Socrates has had praise enough. Neglected are those citizens of Athens—young and old, rich and poor—who were not blinded by appearances. They were so ardently in search of light that they probed his mind or, perhaps it would be more accurate to say that they invited him to probe theirs. "His pupils adored him despite his ugliness and slovenliness. Many of them belonged to Athens' aristocracy, while others were humble people. Some of them became outstanding philosophers, like Euclid, Phaedo, Antisthenes, Aristippus, and Plato, the greatest of them all."[1]

ACQUISITION REQUIRES SHARING

Would we think of Plato as "the greatest of them all" had his insatiable search for truth been blinded by his regard for outward appearances? And what of Aristotle had it not been for the catholicity of Plato. Perhaps he would be unknown to us. And what of you and me were it not for these scalers of the heights? Ortega answers these questions to my satisfaction: "If our thought did not re-think the thought of Descartes, and if Descartes did not re-think the thought of Aristotle, ours would be primitive; we would no longer be the heirs of what has gone before, but would have to go back and begin again. *To surpass is to inherit and to add to.*" An interesting bit of mystery here!

Finally, there is also a mystery as to increasing one's own

[1] See *Treasury of Philosophy,* edited by Dagobert D. Runes, New York, 1955, p. 1111.

wisdom: *continued acquisition requires sharing.* In a word, there is no growth or accretion in wisdom unless that which one receives is freely shared with those who seek. "It is more blessed to give than to receive" simply means that giving or sharing is the prerequisite to receiving. This appears to be the nature of all energy, be it hydraulic, intellectual, spiritual. Sharing, giving off, converts potential energy into moving, power-giving, kinetic energy. This radiant energy, which I do not understand but am aware of, is obviously a flowing phenomenon. As Emerson phrased it, we can only "allow a passage of its beams." It cannot be harbored as a pool within the self. Stagnation!

Numerous individuals have observed that the more they share their ideas with others, the more they receive and the higher grade are their ideas. Why? When one shares, he strives as best he can to perfect his explanations, to put them in the best possible light. Not only do we teach by doing, but best of all, we learn!

In my own case, I have been going over and over these thoughts for years in a struggle for clarity. The ideas are far clearer now than when I began to think about them. Am I any wiser, any closer to truth? Who can be absolutely certain! Yet, sharing with those who care to observe will result in feedbacks and, hopefully, some improvement for me.

20

HOW TO BE
LIKE SOCRATES

*Judge of a man by his questions
rather than by his answers.*
—VOLTAIRE

Like Socrates? Well, not exactly! Each of us is unique. But
the method employed by Socrates to advance understanding
is one that all of us might well try to emulate.

The Socratic method of teaching or discussion is to ask a
series of easily answered questions that inevitably lead the
answerer to a logical conclusion foreseen by the questioner.
This is to teach a student *the way of philosophizing,* as distinguished from urging him to memorize the conclusions of
philosophers.

And what a splendid teaching method this is—quite the
opposite of the popular "compulsory mis-education" which
tends to turn students into carbon copies of so-called teachers. Instead of putting masks on students—blanketing their
minds with someone else's "wisdom"—real teaching is an
unmasking process, helping boys and girls, men and women

133

to find their own hidden aptitudes, potentialities, uniqueness. The teacher and the student experience a togetherness;
they are in harmony or accord. Enlightenment is the mutual
goal.

Why, we must ask, is this superior method so little used?
Why do we not substitute it for the common believe-as-I-do
procedure? It is simply because we do not know the right
questions to ask. Again, why? As Plato suggested, to know
the right questions presupposes an awareness of the correct
answers. Socrates had a knack for this which many others
of us do not. The secret of his achievement? He was wiser
than most of us!

As we can readily discern, to be like Socrates involves
more than a technique for asking questions—generally accepted as the Socratic method. The true skill of Socrates must
be traced further back, to a manner of thinking, a way of
looking at life's role. It is this fountainhead which we must
explore and understand if we are to approximate his achievement, that is, if we are to become wiser.

WHY WORRY ABOUT OTHERS?

In our search for the fountainhead of wisdom let us first
consider why anyone is interested in helping others to unmask themselves, to discover their own aptitudes, potentialities, uniqueness? There are two reasons, both of which are to
be identified with intelligent self-interest.

1. Man is at once an individualistic and a social being. The
higher the development of others, intellectually, morally,

spiritually, the greater is the opportunity for one's own growth in awareness, perception, consciousness—the better to live one's own life. The good life among a den of thieves or in a society of unscrupulous or ignorant people is out of the question.

2. The more one shares his ideas with others the more abundant are his own insights and intuitive flashes, that is, the more numerous and enlightened are his own ideas. This is easily explained: when sharing an idea with another, a man puts his best foot forward—does his utmost—and thus the idea is enriched in his own mind. Enrichment of ideas opens —at least widens—the doors of perception and allows more ideas to flow in. Sharing with others is a means to the perfection of self, one of the steps toward wisdom.

A PHILOSOPHICAL MIDWIFE

A second important aspect of the Socratic fountainhead— another step toward wisdom—is knowing that one knows not. It is axiomatic that a know-it-all cannot learn. Filled to the brim with know-it-all-ness, no room remains for acquisitions; the mind and the soul must remain stagnant. Socrates, reputedly one of the wisest men who ever lived, is famous for his insistence, "I know nothing." This, at first blush, appears to be mere hyperbole; but definitely it is not! Relative to the Infinite Unknown, he was right. Once the mind is freed of know-it-all-ness, knowing pours in, wisdom flourishes.

A third feature of the Socratic fountainhead is both fascinating and instructive—a posture, a way of looking at self and others that anyone can easily emulate.

Socrates, the son of a stonecutter and a midwife, referred to himself as a philosophical midwife. Instead of bringing babies from the womb to the world, he brought truths from obscurity to the minds of seekers. This is to say that he thought of himself as an intellectual go-between, a receiver and a transmitter. He probed the unknown and passed his findings on to those who sought his counsel. A philosophical midwife, indeed!

Now then, if one would be like Socrates, where does he start? Not at the top—the height of wisdom—but at the bottom—training for enlightenment above and beyond where he now stands. Socrates and his method are at the top of the intellectual ladder. I have tried, in the foregoing, to sketch this method from the top of the ladder to its fountainhead. To ascend, one reaches for the bottom rung, learning to serve as philosophical midwife or go-between. To the extent that this is practiced and mastered, to that extent may one rise step by step toward the top.

ANYONE MAY PLAY

At this point I suggest that any normal person can play the role of philosophical midwife; and anyone interested in the improvement of self—in unfoldment—is well advised to do so. I have yet to meet a person from any walk of life, beyond the level of moron, who has not gained some insight, some bit of enlightenment or wisdom which, at least in this respect, makes him outstanding. This may rub off on others without any conscious effort! Unrecognized, this innate ability often lies dormant. But if recognized and consciously developed, it assures individual growth in awareness, perception, consciousness; and this leads in turn toward the good society. The question is, how do we consciously proceed?

The procedure is as simple as it is joyous and gratifying. Merely realize that philosophy is the art of probing the unknown and bringing the findings home in clarity. This is to say that we seek for truth and share it with those who also seek, no two persons ever coming upon precisely the same findings. We enrich or enlighten each other, the hearer as well as the sayer, the teacher perhaps even more than the student. The late C. S. Lewis has enlightened me as I write this. There are situations, he says, where

> The fellow-pupil can help more than the master because he knows less. The difficulty we want him to explain is one he has recently met. The expert met it so long ago that he has forgotten. He sees the whole subject, by now, in such a different light that he cannot conceive what is really troubling the pupil; he sees a dozen other difficulties which ought to be troubling him but aren't.[1]

TO ASSURE SOCIAL HARMONY

Serving as midwife at the birth of new ideas is easily within the competence of anyone; and if enough of us would practice that role we would rid society of conflict and assure social harmony. Why such a confident assertion? Personal experience confirms the truth of this. Merely take note of

---

[1]C. S. Lewis, *Reflections on the Psalms,* London, 1964, p. 9.

your own attitude toward anyone who gives you enlightenment. It is never one of antagonism but, rather, of friendship,
affection, love! I have yet to observe an exception.

Now for the next rung of the ladder. As one succeeds in
probing for truth, he becomes more and more conscious of an
ever-expanding unknown. The more he knows the more he
knows he does not know. If really successful, he will side with
Socrates, "I know I know nothing."[2] In this state of humility,
of standing in awe, knowing flows in, wisdom grows.

INTELLIGENT INTERPRETATION OF SELF-INTEREST

If one can reach the level of humility, of wanting to know,
then the next higher rung of the ladder is within reach: an
intelligent interpretation of self-interest. In reality, this
amounts to an understanding of the Golden Rule: one's interest is never served by doing injury to another.

Immanuel Kant was at this level: no one has a moral right
to do anything that cannot be rationally conceded as a
right to everyone else—the principle of universality. The interest of self and of society are in harmony, not at odds.

William Graham Sumner, also at this level, stated the principle in brilliant terms:

> Every man and woman in society has one big duty. That is,
> to take care of his or her own self. This is a social duty. For,
> fortunately, the matter stands so that the duty of making
> the best of one's self individually is not a separate thing

---

[2]See *Then Truth Will Out, op. cit.,* pp. 21-28.

from the duty of filling one's place in society, but the two are one, and the latter is accomplished when the former is done.[3]

AN EXAMPLE

When it comes to the top rung "in which one asks a series of easily answered questions that inevitably lead the answerer to logical conclusions foreseen by the questioner," I acknowledge incompetence. Yes, I play the role of go-between or midwife of sorts, am aware of knowing nothing, and understand the Golden Rule. However, I do not know enough answers to ask many of the right questions. Why am I not more like Socrates? Simply because I am not wise enough. Nonetheless, each of us can strive for more wisdom and, now and then, some of us may succeed.

The best I can offer is a sampling of the Socratic method— oversimplified for brevity's sake.

Q—*Joe Doakes was lynched. Who did it?*

A—A mob.

Q—*Mob is but a label. Of what is it composed?*

A—Individuals.

Q—*Then did not each individual in the mob lynch Joe Doakes?*

A—That would seem to be the case.

---

[3]William Graham Sumner, *What Social Classes Owe to Each Other,* Caldwell, Idaho, 1954, pp. 97-106.

Q—*Very well. Can any individual gain absolution by committing murder in the name of a label, the mob, a collective?*

A—I guess not.

Q—*Now that we have established that point, let me pose another question. Do you believe in thievery?*

A—Of course not.

Q—*Logically, then, you do not believe that you should use force to take my income to feather your own nest. True or false?*

A—True.

Q—*Is the principle changed if two of you gang up on me?*

A—Not at all.

Q—*One million? Even a majority?*

A—Well, perhaps O.K. if a majority does it.

Q—*Do you mean that might makes right?*

A—Oh, no.

Q—*That is what you have just said. Would you care to retract that?*

A—To be logical, I must.

Q—*You have now agreed that not even 200 million people or any agency thereof—government, labor unions, educational institutions, business firms, or whatever—have a moral right to feather their nests at the expense of others, that is, to advance their own special interests at taxpayers' expense. You have also admitted that no one gains absolution by acting in the name of a collective. Therefore, is not every member who supports or even condones a wrong collective action just as guilty as if he personally committed the act?*

A — I have never thought of it that way before but I now believe you are right.

Thus, by asking the right questions, one may thread his way through the maze of moral, economic, and political philosophy toward truth. This is the method of helping others to find right answers for themselves, the way to truth through their own minds. Your problem and mine is to become wiser that we may increase the number of the right questions to ask.

This, in my view, is the way to become more and more like Socrates.

21

VOICES IN THE WILDERNESS

A man's humanity depends on how deeply he gains guidance through listening.

—KARL JASPERS

Isaiah's phrase of some 27 centuries ago was applied to John the Baptist: "a voice crying in the wilderness." That phrasing persists as self-description in the minds of those whose devoted efforts go unheeded. For most of the present-day minority who oppose our plunge into socialism are saying, if not to others at least to themselves, "We are only voices crying in the wilderness."

Is the metaphor an apt one, as currently used? Cries are heard, yes, but they are cries of despair—which may, in no small measure, account for the fateful resignation so much observed around us.

Further, the despair rests upon the dubious supposition that ours are voices of enlightenment within a wilderness, that is, among multitudes who do not or cannot hear our wise messages. "We are only talking to ourselves!" But this may

142

be an occasion that calls for joyousness, not depression, for activity of mind, not resignation. At least the thought merits examination.

Voices? Let each of us examine his own voice for content and clarity and then render an honest, unbiased judgment. Simply put yourself in the position of those not of our turn of mind. How much ear would you or I give to our respective voices? Honest self-assessment results in a judgment that falls short of flattery—for me, at any rate.

It has been truly said, "a man will not be interested if you tell him that he can acquire by long and difficult work something which, in his opinion, he already has." Talking to myself, I muse: long and difficult work ahead for me after all of these years of effort, and rarely much in doubt about my own understanding? Yes, this is the answer I get upon careful self-examination.

SELF-APPRAISAL

There have been many capable thinkers over the centuries who have stressed the difficulty—the near impossibility—of standing off from oneself and having an unbiased look, seeing the self as others do. Robert Burns gave this problem a pretty phrasing:

> Oh wad some power the giftie gie us
> To see oursels as others see us!

Whatever be this power, the "giftie" it confers is an awakening from a slumber featured by dreams of self-satisfaction —a rather rude awakening!

With this feat accomplished, what do I find? First, an evaluation of self more realistic than it was, if not quite so satisfying. And, second, a relocated wilderness. Instead of regarding the wilderness as "out there," think of it as within me! How is it now? The wilderness is not comprised of countless others who supposedly cannot hear; it is a personal bewilderment reflected in a voice not skilled enough to attract many listeners. What a new face this puts on our problem! At the very least, it sets the stage for long and difficult work, the kind of undertaking that has the possibility of some accomplishment; whereas, the other way is doomed to failure. There is joy in headway, only frustration in fruitless effort.

FICKLE PUBLIC OPINION

Before dealing further with my own bewilderment and such correction as is possible, let me clarify for myself one point about the "out there," the wilderness where persons confront each other. True, it is the majority viewpoint or consensus that determines what goes on in society: the quality of men elected to public office, the kind of legislation passed, the degree of statism or freedom, the extent of coercive practices or violence that private groups can inflict, and so on. However, I am certain to be drawn off course unless I carefully assess what really constitutes a society's prevailing viewpoint or consensus. The appearance it gives of numerical strength is only the froth and not the brewing agent, the foam and not the starter. The brewing agent—the stuff itself—is thought, idea, be it true or false. *To say that the consensus rests on solid opinions by as much as one per cent of the population is probably an exaggeration.*

The overwhelming majority of citizens have no well-grounded opinions, no thought-out ideas, on the subject of our concern. They merely lean toward or follow this or that ideological camp. For the most part, their allegiance follows impulsive acquiescence in cliches, attractive personalities, party labels, how the wind blows, and other forces lacking in idea content. Only lights of unprecedented brilliance can cause any of them to turn their eyes toward freedom. And, then, at best, only a few!

THE REMNANT

The few—The Remnant—are all who count. They are, as Albert Jay Nock observed, an odd lot: quiet, shy of show-offs; indeed, they will have nothing to do with them. These few—mostly unknowns—*are the ones who tip the scales,* and their search is always for those who, to some extent, make progress against their own bewilderment, who gain in understanding and clarity of expression, who evidence integrity and, above all, who try to enlighten themselves. Those of The Remnant "run a mile" from reformers; they resent all attempts at "ramming ideas down their necks." This attests to their realism for they know the futility of such an effort; it simply cannot be done.[1]

---

[1]The Remnant is dramatized in *Isaiah's Job* by Albert Jay Nock. I read this essay 36 years ago. It gave me my first instruction in the methods appropriate to freedom. As the Bible from which the story is taken, it merits reading again and again. Copy on request from Foundation for Economic Education, Irvington, N.Y. 10533.

A man's life is his own—and his Maker's—inalienable, nontransferable. It may be devoted or given to an ideal, or to an idea, but cannot be transplanted into another living being. This is to say that my ideas or yours cannot be implanted in another—except at that other's bidding or doing. If there is to be a transmission of ideas, the exchange occurs by the will and action of the receiver. And he draws into himself only that which he sees and values. I can perceive an idea, perhaps; but the idea itself is blind to me, can enter my mind only by my conscious effort and acceptance. The simplicity of this process is recognized by those rare individuals who comprise The Remnant. They are forever in search of light; and they are the ones who matter in the continuous upward struggle of man toward a better society.

EDUCATION VERSUS ENTERTAINMENT

These truisms bring into focus a problem that perplexes many devotees of freedom: the general apathy, the paralysis of thought in our time. Without question, the vast majority of Americans spend many of their leisure hours viewing TV. This tends to put their lives on a nonintellectual level, as does the energy they devote to idle conversation and limited reading of serious material.

Such low forms of communication enormously influence participants to lean toward or to acquiesce in ways of life quite the opposite of freedom and self-responsibility. The winds of opinion blow in the wrong direction. And the reason for the wrong direction is usually ascribed to our failure to put the freedom message over the same channels or through the same media. The argument is that we should compete at this level. But I doubt that this gets at the educational problem we face.

TV and the like are, for the most part, entertainment media, and our objective is not entertainment. True, much nonsense can be blended with entertainment because the audience is not viewing, listening, reading for philosophical and ideological enlightenment. With no higher aim than merriment and diversion, the millions can indeed be blown in nonsensical directions. As Jacques Barzun phrases it, ". . . unless we *consciously* resist, the nonsense does not pass by us but into us." And I would add, unless we *consciously* try, the truth will not pass into us but will pass us by. Whenever *conscious* effort is lacking, people are easy and natural victims of the current winds that blow; they can be sold nonsense!

OURS NOT A SELLING PROBLEM

Ours, however, is not a selling problem either, which is to say that no one has ever been "blown" into enlightenment. The gaining of understanding, knowledge, wisdom is, instead, a do-it-yourself, gathering-in project.

I am becoming more and more convinced that any reversal of the societal trend calls for a radical approach or strategy. Otherwise, we will continue to resort to means and methods that are useless if not downright mischievous.

Let us now face up to the nature and enormity of our problem. A philosopher whose thoughts I admire asserted: "The known is what's no longer a problem." This appears to be true in one sense, yet false in another: the unknown has not yet been recognized as the problem. Our societal disarray, for instance, is no problem to an animal, to a person in slumber, or to the millions who are in a state of unawareness—the addicts of merriment and diversion. What does this mean to the thoughtful individual who is bent on the freedom way of life?

It means that he must advance his own enlightenment to such a brilliance that a few, at least, will turn away from the TV and other entertainment to an enlightenment effort of their own. Never in the history of mankind have the distractions been more high-powered and glamorous than now. Nor, by the same token, has so much been required in the way of personal excellence to turn the trend toward freedom. *To succeed, we must excel those who have gone before us!* Personally, I would not have it any other way; this is a challenge worthy of any man who sees life's purpose as growth in consciousness.

WHAT CAN I DO?

Now to my own bewilderment and its correction. What shows forth as the obvious first step? What should my ambition be? To make of myself a prophet, a seer, one who is to enlighten mankind? Indeed, not! Any such aim is self-defeating. I must aspire to be a man, not a god. To concentrate on the latter would erase all chances of achieving the former. Further, no one who really counts in the upgrading struggle ever searches for light from those afflicted with egomania. I desire only what man's freedom opens up to him. ". . . *an opportunity to become that which he can authentically be.*"

What can I authentically be? A seeker bent on enlightenment! Where will that take me? Heaven only knows! But this I do know: no one who counts will ever look to me for light unless I have enlightenment to share.

The answer emerges in crystal clarity: try as best I can to qualify for membership in that odd lot, The Remnant—a seeker after light. A voice crying in the wilderness? No, quite the opposite—one listening for enlightened voices: the voice within, and from others, past and present, voices that may lead me, even if haltingly, out of my own bewilderment. Who knows! I may see the dawn and, if I do, a few others will see it with me.

22

OPEN VERSUS
CLOSED MINDS

I had six honest serving men.
They taught me all I knew.
Their names were Where and What and When—
And Why and How and Who.

— **KIPLING**

Open-mindedness is almost everywhere hailed as a virtue, especially in "educated" circles. A person of closed mind, on the other hand, is generally condemned as narrow, shallow, nit-witted. I had accepted these generalities until recently when a philosopher friend asked, "You are not open-minded about everything, are you?" I knew instantly and answered "No!" But this, of course, poses the question: To what should one's mind be closed and to what should it be open?

As a starter, I would like my mind open to truths yet to be perceived and closed to all nonsense. Were one's mind open to everything, he would reject experience; for example, he might explore the principle of gravitation anew by trying to walk on air over a deep ditch. He would forever be uncertain whether honesty were the best policy. Maybe yes and maybe no. A slave to open-mindedness! My mind is absolutely closed on these matters of gravity and honesty; and, on examination, I find it closed to a host of other propositions.

While no one knows overmuch, each of us knows some things or he would perish from the earth. A good rule: Close the mind on what one knows and understands and keep it open to what is not known and understood. In either function, one's mind serves him as a guide to life's fulfillment, helping him to avoid the ditches and stay on the road toward his destination.

This way of looking at "mindedness" presents a seeming anomaly. It had never occurred to me before that the more one knows and understands, the more the issues upon which his mind is closed! But although a closed mind may indicate the number of issues upon which a man has reflected and reached settled conclusions, it also might be a sign that one has perceived next to nothing. The degree of closed-mindedness is not necessarily an accurate guage of how much one knows and understands!

IS THE MIND WORKING?

The lesson? Never try to estimate the knowledge and wisdom of others by how closed or open their minds. Any estimate of this kind should be confined to self and then only after every possible thought has been explored to determine whether or not one is on sound ground. In other words, a person's mind may be closed with something in it, things which he knows or sincerely believes and upon which he can act; or it may be closed and quite empty, receptive to no ideas at all.

By the same token, a mind may be open, but open to every kind of an idea—wise or foolish; or it may be so open on every side that no idea can be registered there for reference or use. So the question is not entirely whether a mind is open or closed but whether it is a working mind and, if so, to what purpose.

The idea that one's mind should be open to that which is not known or understood and that our aim is to grow in knowledge and wisdom, gives rise to a logical and relevant question. How may we best serve each other as each of us pursues this end? *By opening our minds to each other!* By so doing, we expose what light we have gained and, thus, maximize the total enlightenment. Open-mindedness in its best sense!

Unquestionably, this sharing process accounts for the greater expanse of knowledge and wisdom today than existed among the Neanderthals or Cro-Magnon man. Far more than is generally realized, we have inherited from the past; we ride on the shoulders of its giants! We are free to pick their brains, so to speak, to whatever extent we are willing to open our minds to their ideas. Likewise, we may pick the brains of one another among our contemporaries to the extent each is willing, always bearing in mind the personal responsibility to choose and judge which ideas to accept or reject, and which of ours are worthy of sharing with others.

EXPLORING THE UNKNOWN

As Ortega phrased it, "The known is what's no longer a problem." So numerous and all-pervasive are our problems that the unknown must be regarded as infinite—never-ending. Those issues to which the mind is still open are problems rather than answers and can hardly be shared as knowledge. Thus, the best one can do for others is to enumerate those ideas and propositions on which his own mind is closed— express what he believes to be true. There follows a sampling of what I have in mind. "Here I stand, I can do no other."

1. The Golden Rule and the Ten Commandments.
2. The good society rests on individuals having high moral scruples and ethical guidelines; no organizational gadgetry, however deftly devised, can overcome moral and ethical deficiencies.
3. Government limited to administering justice and keeping the peace—equality before the law—is an essential adjunct to morality. Anarchy—each a law unto himself —is not a viable social philosophy.
4. Government—organized force—can only inhibit, restrain, penalize. It has no business interfering in the creative realm.
5. Creativity stems exclusively from individuals acting privately, competitively, cooperatively, voluntarily.
6. No man who lives, no association, nor any government is competent to decide for any other where he shall work, what his hours or wage shall be, what and with whom he may exchange, or what thoughts he shall entertain.
7. Freedom in transactions is an absolute principle.
8. The value of any good or service is what another will give in willing exchange.
9. The good or bad politician is not the cause of good or bad government. He reflects the thinking of his con-

stituents. When the thinking is good enough, then good men can and will be elected to office.

10. Obedience to one's highest conscience is to seek approval from God, not men.

A final thought: There is a reliable test as to whether or not one's closed-mindedness derives from a growing knowledge or from a lack of understanding. If from lack, there will be a sense of know-it-all-ness; if from growth, the more issues on which one's mind is closed, the better paved is his access to the unknown. This test merely emphasizes the obvious: the more one knows, the more is he aware of the unknown—the challenge!

23

LEADERSHIP REDEFINED

Allur'd to brighter worlds, and led the way.
—OLIVER GOLDSMITH

Both saints and villians are found in the pages of history. The former are credited with leading us in the ways of virtue, while the latter lead us toward evil. In my opinion, we are caught in an aged word trap whenever we think of leadership in these terms, and this causes untold mischief. Accordingly, I offer the following definition and explanation of leadership. Conceded, it is novel, for it has no dictionary or other authority. Just an idea that makes sense to me.

Imagine a dozen climbers scaling the Matterhorn; the one leading the way would doubtless be the most skilled and knowledgeable of the lot. As to this venture, we would regard him as a leader.

Let us now assume that once atop the mountain disaster strikes; the climbers slip and fall to their doom. We would ascribe no leadership qualities whatsoever to the first man to fall.

By this analogy, I wish to suggest that leadership in our world of social affairs must be associated *only* with achievement, attainment, progress and *never* with a fall from grace. The man out front is a leader when showing the ways to higher goals; he is not a leader when in the vanguard of social degradations.

Why dwell on this? Individuals, if long on energy and short on humility, aspire to positions of leadership. To them there is no greater gratification of the ego than to have others think of them as leading the way, shaping the lives of others, directing the course of human events. Getting out in front of "the wave of the future" is all that is required for such an evaluation, and it matters not how degrading the movement.

SIGNS THAT MISLEAD US

Even though most Americans frown on Nazism, they still regard Hitler as having exerted leadership. But if leadership were associated only with righteous and uplifting efforts, his actions exhibited no leadership qualities. False notions of leadership are quashed by recognition that dictatorship is a disreputable business. Who would wish to be a dictator—indeed, who could—were everyone to scorn or look down upon that position? Traces of the domineering habit in the mill run of us, along with other reasons, may cause us to follow and thus lend unwarranted encouragement to these dominators. Straighten out our understanding of leadership, and we will take a big step toward correcting this mischief.

Even had Hitler designed Nazism, he would not qualify as a leader any more than would the designer of nasty words.

pornography, a muck heap, or any other degradation. As the first one among climbers falling to their doom, Hitler was the victim of circumstances not of his making. He was a follower of evil forces he did not understand.

Should we not realize that whatever shows forth on the political horizon, in the U.S.A. or elsewhere, is no more than a reflection or echoing of the preponderant thinking at the time? If the consensus be sheer babble, then the best babbler among us will be out front.

Hitler did not design Nazism; to repeat, he was its victim, a follower fully sold on its nonsense. He found himself in the vanguard by reason of being the noisiest, most energetic, egotistic, charismatic of all the victims. He did not lead Germany into that catastrophe; the low-grade thinking was responsible. It was the ignoble thoughts that made Hitler Der Führer!

INTO SOCIAL DISASTER

Be it Nazism, fascism, Fabianism, communism, socialism, welfarism, the planned economy—any arrangement that calls for coercive control over the creative actions of citizens—these are social disasters, retrogression from the nearest approximation to freedom ever attained: the politico-economic situation that once distinguished America.

No moral, intellectual, spiritual, political, economic decline has ever had a leader—nothing but one of the followers out front. Keep in mind that the politicians who are in the vanguard of these movements are but the victims of a deteriorating consensus.

A leader not only is "allur'd to brighter worlds" but to some extent scales the heights. He is the seeker and finder of more enlightenment, one who by concentration, study, insights, integrity, humility, and devotion to truth leads himself and, hopefully, others of us out of the wilderness. For, as Mencius phrased it, "Never a man who has bent himself been able to make others straight."

By definition, leaders are persons who come upon new and, thus, unaccustomed thoughts. It is for this reason that leaders are rarely known in their own time. The fruit of their labors may not be recognized until years later, sometimes centuries, often never.

Theorists of authoritarianism—Marx, for instance—or its political horn tooters—Hitler, Stalin, and some local examples— are immediately celebrated; they are in the headlines. The real probers of modern times—Adam Smith, Bastiat, Menger, Mises, to name a few—will someday be known as we now know Socrates, Epictetus, and others of the ancient world.

An interesting thought intrudes itself: the leaders of our time are obscure and must be sought by us precisely as they, to be leaders, must search for truth. May we find them as they find truth! In any event, let us never think of anyone as a leader who is not scaling the heights. If we get our definition of leadership correct, the horn tooters will lose their celebrity —will no longer occupy the limelight—and, thus, the leaders and their enlightened thoughts will be that much easier to find.

24

MR. ANONYMOUS

The hottest places in hell are reserved for those who, in a period of moral crisis, maintain their neutrality.

—DANTE

In pondering the matter of anonymity, I came to these conclusions: In matters of charity it is a mark of virtue for a man to resort to anonymity; but as related to a rapidly growing authoritarianism, it is disgraceful for a man to retreat behind namelessness. Our actions here have a great deal to do with societal well-being, a point that is generally overlooked. When and when not to employ anonymity is linked to political economy, which makes this subject anything but esoteric or "cloud 9"; it is a down-to-earth matter.

The explanations to follow are in support of these contentions:

1. State welfarism grows and eventually takes over when the closely related concepts of voluntary exchange and Judeo-Christian charity are neither understood nor practiced.

2. The state planned and operated economy proliferates
when citizens refuse to speak their minds in their own
name.

Anonymity is an absolute prerequisite to true charity; it is
utter folly to think we can preserve a market economy and
stem authoritarianism anonymously. We are faced with
silently practicing what is right in our concern for the unfortunate and with openly proclaiming what we believe to be
right in our economic and political relationships. Regret-
fully, the tendency is just the opposite: proclaiming our benefactions to all and sundry and silencing our thoughts when
not in accord with popular notions. Most of us deserve self-
censure on both counts!

My title is that of a biographical book about the late William Volker.[1] Arriving in the U.S.A. as a young man from
Germany, he began work at one dollar a week. Young William, deeply religious, was charitable to those in need and did
his best to remain anonymous. He lived to a ripe old age and
all of his business ventures were outstanding successes; he
gave many millions to charity—a third of his vast earnings.
The man must have done something right, that is, lived in
harmony with a sound principle!

CHARITY IN SECRET

Anonymity as related to charity is a biblical instruction:
"Let not thy left hand know what thy right hand doeth."

One does not have to believe that every word in the Bible

---

[1]Herbert C. Cornuelle, *Mr. Anonymous,* Caldwell, Idaho, 1951.

is true as written to discern the correctness of this admonition. Why give and forget you gave? Why toss one's benefactions out of mind? Simple: it is the preventative of a psychic illness: self-adulation. Admittedly, it is not easy to forget a kindness one has bestowed but it is worth trying. Indeed, unless forgotten, credit to self—pride—is the result. "The charity that hastens to proclaim its good deeds," said William Hutton, "ceases to be charity, and is only pride and ostentation."

No question about it, one should learn not to dwell upon—better to forget instantly—his own benefactions. But why keep the recipient in the dark? Must anonymity be carried this far? Of course! Otherwise, the thanks and gratitude will come bouncing back so that the left hand cannot help but know what the right hand doeth. Worse yet, the recipient will feel an indebtedness which transforms the intended helping hand into a hand seeking praise. Further, this may leave the beneficiary demanding more.

THE RISE OF WELFARISM

True, the understanding of Judeo-Christian charity requires a high level of wisdom and its practice an extremely sensitive performance. But even so, why is it heeded so rarely? Or, perhaps a better question, why does it seem to me to be a virtue headed for extinction? My answer: the rise of state welfarism! Were Judeo-Christian charity the vogue, or even if it had a respectable observation and practice, coercive welfarism would be clearly recognized as an economic perversion and "laughed out of court." The decline of true charity is proportional to the rise in state welfarism, presently on the rampage.[2]

Why do I refer to state welfarism as an economic perversion? Simply because the "have-nots" whom it is supposed to help at the expense of the "haves" are the very ones who bear the brunt of it!

DOING ONE ANOTHER'S LAUNDRY

To the extent that the members of society are engrossed in the political process of doing one another's laundry, there is little prospect that anyone would bother to invent and build a washing machine or open a laundromat. Welfare programs, based inevitably on steeply graduated income taxes, destroy the incentive and the capacity to save and invest in the tools and facilities that create job opportunities and permit mass production—for the masses. Every dollar's worth of potential capital investment taxed out of the market in the name of "welfarism" closes the gates of the market place to innumerable poor consumers who otherwise might have been able to buy what each most wants instead of what a government official thinks each needs.

The "have-nots" are the ones who substantially foot the bill by reason of their scanty supply of dollars having less and less purchasing power. However, hardly any among the "have-nots" realize that they are victims of state welfarism

---

[2]As state welfarism increases, anonymity—a requirement of true charity—becomes more and more impossible. We are increasingly compelled to report our gifts to government and such information becomes public, not private, property.

and even less do they relate this economic perversion to the waning of Judeo-Christian charity. This is the point that we need to stand for and to explain, openly and personally, proclaiming to all the world the blessings of freedom.

The above suggests the case for anonymity in charitable activities, the virtuous practice of which is declining. Now for the case against anonymity where its enormous practice is utterly disgraceful. Edmund Burke's observation is excellent background for what follows:

> The only thing necessary for the triumph of evil is for good men to do nothing.

The Mr. Anonymous of the disgraceful variety is more of an *it* than a *he*! Why this assessment? Such individuals are self-neutered, that is, they run away from personal identification —hide behind false fronts. A nasty letter unsigned is this trait in its most loathsome form. But equally anonymous and useless is "the name used by an author in place of his true name": pen name, nom de plume, pseudonym, alias, and the like. Whatever the thought expressed, it is authored by a nobody; it lacks endorsement, is without authority.

HIDING BEHIND PSEUDONYMS

This same kind of anonymity extends into the politico-economic realm. Millions of citizens refuse to stick their necks out by publicly standing up for their private convictions. Hiding behind pseudonyms, these people run away from the responsibility of identifying themselves with any issue under fire; they let the committee, the organization, or

political collectives speak while they—the faint-hearted ones—
remain anonymous. There are today, during a moral and economic crisis in human affairs, no more than a very small
minority who in their own names are speaking, writing, and
standing for what is right about private property and voluntary exchange, and what is wrong about coercive intervention
and unlimited government.

Bear in mind that righteousness in any area whatever must
remain unknown and without support except as it is pronounced and affirmed by discrete individuals who are openly
linking their reputation and the sacredness of their names to
the truth as they see it. Righteousness is but a cosmic whisper
unless brought to earthly use by some individual ready and
willing to stake his reputation on it. In the absence of such
open and proud integrity, rightness has no muscle, no one nor
any thing to support it; there is only a vacuum into which
nonsense flows, there being no resistance.

I repeat, the state-planned and operated economy proliferates when citizens refuse to speak their minds in their own
name.

Mr. Anonymous, let us know what brand of anonymity you
practice that we may know the quality of your citizenship.
Or, better yet, let me examine and understand and make clear
what kind of a citizen I am.

25

THE CONNOISSEUR
IN SOCIETY

So act that your principle of action
might safely be made a law for the
whole world.

—KANT

According to Jefferson there are those among men who comprise a natural aristocracy based upon virtue and talent—an elite order having extraordinary intellectual, ethical, personal, and spiritual qualities. Persons so graced are not necessarily to be found among those of rank and power, that is, among aristocrats as the term is commonly used. The rare ones who should elicit our admiration are a very special breed of distinguished exemplars.

These natural aristocrats emerge, not because of their efforts to influence others, but because they work to realize their own fulfillment. They stand out naturally among men simply by manifesting their acquired virtues, talents, disciplines, and not because they strive for the limelight. Any other stance would be alien to their nature. Thus, the *natural* aristocracy!

The presence of such an order of persons makes for a good society, and the societal situation with which we are concerned—of maximum individual liberty—improves or deteriorates as the natural aristocracy flourishes or wanes. A natural aristocracy in the pink of condition sets the standard or tone by which we harmonize and prosper. But when the leaders in business, religion, politics, education fall from rectitude, then society is beset by antagonisms, conflict, discord, nonsense.

Conceded, a natural aristocracy in the pink of condition is the prime requirement for a good society. But we should take note of this: such an aristocracy seems to flourish or wane in the presence or absence of connoisseurs—those with a taste for excellence. In the absence of connoisseurs, exemplars are no more to be expected than is a supply of beautiful paintings for exhibition only to the blind. Without a demand for virtue and talents, there can be no excellence, no exemplars.

How, then, are exemplars and connoisseurs to be distinguished? I am beginning to suspect that they are one and the same! With respect to gastronomy, for instance, it is obvious that there would be no chefs of the *cordon bleu* excellence were there no connoisseurs of food; nor would there be any of the latter without the former. If my suspicion is well-founded, then we cannot ask which comes first, the chicken or the egg. In pondering this seeming anomaly, a verse by Dryden comes to mind:

We first make our habits, and then our habits make us.
All habits gather by unseen degrees,
As brooks make rivers, rivers run to seas.

Would there be any seas without the brooks and rivers? Unlikely! Nor would there be any brooks and rivers without the seas. What goes on here? The sun evaporates the seas, gathering as moisture in the heavens. Condensed, it falls to earth draining into brooks and rivers and they, in turn, run to the seas. Now ask the question, what comes first? This has no answer for it is a cyclical phenomenon such as the orbit of a heavenly body. It is a continuum: "a continuous whole . . . things whose parts cannot be separated."[1]

CAUSE AND EFFECT

These observations and reflections lead me to believe that exemplars and connoisseurs cannot be arranged as first and second; they coexist, mutually serving one another as cause-and-effect. So, do not expect excellence without a taste for it, or vice versa. These twin attributes ascend and decline in unison precisely as do the left and right wings of a bird in flight.

This view, I realize, may be questioned. For all sorts of persons think of themselves as connoisseurs of this or that while having no skills of their own. There are, for instance, self-styled connoisseurs of art who cannot paint a barn, of cooking who cannot scramble an egg, of writing who cannot phrase a sentence, of political economy who cannot distinguish the free from the rigged market. Such lopsidedness between taste on the one hand and exemplarity on the other reflects self-deception. Actions speak louder than words:

[1]For an artistic treatment of this phenomenon see "You Cannot Pick a Dandelion" by Arthur P. Moor, *The Freeman,* April 1964.

"For as he thinketh in his heart, so is he." (Proverbs 23:7)

Applying such judgment to myself, what do I find? I am no better a connoisseur of golf than I am a golfer, of cooking than I am a chef, of painting than I am an artist, of poetry than I am a poet. True, I profess to like or dislike certain dishes at the table, certain art, music, poetry, or what have you. But such responses are, for the most part, only feelings, not taste in its refined, exalted sense. In no instance am I more connoisseur than exemplar!

In short, exemplarity and an exalted taste for excellence go hand in hand; however, neither one comes first. So, how and where do we begin?

ONE MUST TAKE A STAND

Before suggesting *how* and *where* we should begin, perhaps it might be well further to explain *why* we should begin. In what respect, really, does the natural aristocrat so remarkably distinguish himself from the mill run of us? The quick answer is that each person among the mill run of us is guided by exterior authority as distinguished from the natural aristocrat who is guided by interior authority. Most of us are directed by expediencies as is a committee which rarely if ever is right, while the natural aristocrat is directed by reason and conscience which assures the closest possible alignment with rightness. Let me elaborate.

First, what is right? It is what one's highest conscience dictates as right. While this in fact may not be truth, it is as close to truth as anyone can at any given moment attain.

Second, why is a committee rarely if ever right? Simply

because its conclusions or resolutions are an amalgam, compromise, potpourri of the members' varying conceptions of what ought to be done. The final position is whatever a majority finds not too offensive; in few instances is it strictly in accord with what any single conscience dictates as right. A committee can rarely be right unless one endorses the naive notion that might makes right or, its equivalent, that whatever a majority endorses is right.

Third, in what respect do persons among the mill run of us resemble a committee and, thus, fail to stand for what is right? Most of our proclaimed positions are divorced from and are not dictated by highest conscience. Instead, they are determined by the circumstances which surround the person: pressures, popular opinions, cliches, fear of disapproval, desire for fame, wealth, power, and so on. As in the case of committee resolutions, proclaimed positions are, for the most part, no more than an amalgam, compromise, potpourri of environmental circumstances. *Truth—what's right—is not to be found in this!*

FORMING A HABIT

Now, how and where to begin that we may become at once a connoisseur and an exemplar? Dryden's sentence gives us the cue: "We first make our habits, and then our habits make us." *I* make *my* habits and *you* make *yours!* In a word, my habits can be made to respond to my own will. The Reverend Edmund A. Opitz enlightens us along these lines:

Man is not God; he does not *create* himself, nor write the

laws of his own being; but men do *make* themselves. And as they do so, they begin to discover who they are and what they may become. "That wonderful structure, Man," wrote Edmund Burke, "whose prerogative it is to be in a great degree a creature of his own working, and who, when made as he ought to be made, is destined to hold no trivial place in the creation."

There we have it! This is to say that if one so wills it, he can make a natural aristocrat of himself. And the habit grows on itself; that is, the twin attributes—exemplarity and the taste for excellence—will become habitual, a natural way of life.

The launching, getting off the ground, that initial phase requiring will power, is simple enough to phrase if not to accomplish. Merely resolve, *whatever the circumstances or pressures,* that everything approved or condoned accurately reflects whatever one's highest conscience dictates as right. True, we have to live in the world as it is. This fact, however, should in no way adulterate our proclaimed positions. Whoever expresses them in purity is a connoisseur in society, and as his taste for excellence sharpens, so will his exemplary service to the rest of us.

26

THE INMOST AND
THE OUTMOST

*. . . the inmost in due time becomes
the outmost.*

—**EMERSON**

The employment of these opposites—the inmost and the outmost—to dramatize a fundamental societal problem, is Emerson's invention, not mine, but they have an important bearing on some personal concerns.

It is my firm conviction that man's earthly purpose is
growth in awareness, perception, consciousness. I believe
that man, millennia hence, is intended to excel us in this
respect precisely as men of our time are markedly ahead of
Neanderthalers. Each of us is here to play his part in this
growth; not to stay put; not to rot on the vine. This is the way
I read the Cosmic Intention, and I accept this reading as my
basic premise. Such a premise undeniably requires individual liberty for its realization.

The attainment of liberty demands a two-part understanding: (1) a grasp of the ideology itself, and (2) an awareness of the appropriate method for achieving it. I believe ours is primarily a learning problem, rather than an exercise in selling; it follows that the methodology is even more important than the ideology. Were all individuals devoted to their own improvement—increasing their awareness, knowledge, upgrading their understanding—there would not be a seeker after power among us. And in the absence of coercionists there could be no authoritarianism, none whatsoever! Individual liberty prevails in a society where no one lords it over others, and the person tending to his own growth feels no need to rule others. Hence, the importance of choosing the correct method for advancing liberty, lest we waste effort and aggravate the very problem we would settle.

INCREASING ONE'S CANDLE POWER

Enlightenment—increasing one's own candle power—and sharing one's findings with others, has long been my idea of correct method. Emerson put it thus:

> Speak your latent conviction, and it shall be the universal sense; *for the inmost in due time becomes the outmost.* . . . Familiar as the voice of the mind is to each, the highest merit we ascribe to Moses, Plato and Milton is that they set at naught books and traditions, but spoke what *they* thought.[1]

---

[1] Ralph Waldo Emerson, *Compensation and Self-Reliance,* Westwood, N.J., p. 31.

Anyone familiar with the works of Emerson is well aware that what he wrote and spoke were *his* thoughts. I would emulate him—in this respect, at least—for what follows are *my* thoughts concerning his thoughts.

The method of self-improvement is not popular. For instance, this morning's mail brings a typical criticism, one which helps to draw my thesis into focus:

> You've written that a candle's light can be seen miles away in the dark of space. But when the enemy is exploding skyrockets, that light can't be seen. You are one of the few with vast training in matters of freedom; yet you insist on being a remote, hermit-like wise man, not showing his wares in the great market place where men buy so readily so many false values, for that's all they see around them. You do a great work, but against the opposition, it is pale and puny, and it could be colorful and grow tremendously.

No question about it, this man is a devotee of freedom. Ideology, splendid! But what is his method for advancing individual liberty? It is one of confrontation. Argue the rascals down! He believes that the outmost governs the inmost, whereas, I contend the very opposite is true. We hear a clap of thunder, but the genesis of this noise is a gigantic electrical spark which creates a sudden vacuum into which air rushes. The thunder, as the outmost, is a consequence. I say, look to the spark and not the thunder for, as Emerson suggests, "the inmost in due time becomes the outmost."

In the area of our concern—political economy—what is the outmost? It is, in substance, the policy of the state, as described by the eminent Swiss psychiatrist, Carl Jung. A few of his pertinent comments:

. . . the policy of the state . . . is thrust upon the individual from outside and consists in the execution of an abstract idea which ultimately tends to attract all life to itself. . . . The individual is increasingly deprived of the moral decision as to how he should live his own life, and instead is ruled, fed, clothed and educated as a social unit, accommodated in the appropriate housing unit, and amused in accordance with the standards that give pleasure and satisfaction to the masses. The rulers, in their turn, are just as much social units as the ruled and are distinguished only by the fact that they are specialized mouthpieces of the State doctrine. . . . They are more likely, however, to be the slaves of their fictions. . . . They merely function as a megaphone for collective opinion. . . . The State in particular is turned into a quasi-animate personality from whom everything is expected. In reality, it is only a camouflage for those individuals who know how to manipulate it.[2]

Admittedly, it is the outmost—the runaway policy of the state, the collective opinion—that grabs our attention and urges upon us its reform. However, unless we discern that the outmost is effect and not cause, we will waste our labors by tinkering with the megaphone, touching up the camouflage, substituting one clap of thunder for another. As fruitless as repairing an echo!

The current consensus, the effect that so deeply concerns all devotees of the freedom philosophy, is but an echo of mass nonsense, voices not "of the mind" but of the lower passions.

---

[2]Carl G. Jung, *The Undiscovered Self,* New York, 1958, pp. 13-18.

The voice of the mind—yours or mine—is not a noise but a light. If we abhor the present consensus, then look to our own lights. Bear in mind that neither lights nor their reflections can be shouted down. Witness the lights of Moses, Plato, Milton, Emerson, Jung, Socrates, Epictetus, Montaigne, Adam Smith, Bastiat, Mises, and a host of others. Their lights are brilliant as ever. But they go unseen by eyes diverted from self-enlightenment and turned fruitlessly toward echo repairing.

CHASING ECHOES

Appraised in this manner, it seems plain that the believers in individual liberty who concentrate their energies on combatting echoes unwittingly become parties to the very condition they would remedy. For, by taking this wrong course, they reject the right one, namely, the search after light. No one can go in two directions at once. For this reason, the reflection—the outmost—is just that much dimmer than would otherwise be the case. Indeed, a substantial reason for our present plight is an unawareness of how nonsense is dispelled or, conversely, of how awakening is achieved.

Let us approach this matter from another angle. Why do people by the millions, in and out of politics, lord it over others? Parents over children and vice versa? Husbands over wives and vice versa? Employees over employers and vice versa? Politicians over citizens and vice versa? From whence comes this dictatorial penchant? What accounts for it? Some insist that it is a natural, instinctive trait of the human being; others say it is rooted in fear.

To Hobbes men were brutes so life degenerated into a perpetual condition of "war against every other" in a struggle not just to survive . . . but to dominate his fellows. For man is possessed of "a perpetual and restless desire of power after power that ceaseth only in death." President Wilson pressed for "self determination" as a right of all people after World War I on the assumption that they wanted to rule themselves. According to Hobbes, they want to rule each other. . . . Adam Smith suggests that this lust for power may be the principal motive for slavery: "The pride of man makes him love to domineer. . . ."[3]

UNAWARENESS, THE PROBLEM

I am convinced that what we call a lust for power does not stem from any of these "causes" but, basically, from *unawareness*. It is a weakness more than a lust; men resort to force because they do not know any better. With notable exceptions, men are:

  a. unaware of how little they know. Without such awareness, they can envision a better world only as others are carbon copies of themselves. The remedy? Cast others in their image, by force, if necessary.
  b. unaware that our infinite variation in talents and virtues merits approval and not censure, for variation is implicit in the Cosmic Order. Were all identical, all would perish.
  c. unaware of an inability to mold the life of another beneficially. Each individual has but the dimmest no-

---

[3]See "When Men Appeal From Tyranny to God" by Edward Coleson, *The Freeman,* June 1972.

tion of his own miraculous being; about others he knows substantially nothing. Man is *not* the Creator!

d. unaware that consciousness is ultimately the single, primal reality. The world and all it embraces, be it your world or mine, comes into focus only in the eyes of the beholder. Our respective worlds are those of which we are conscious—no more, no less!

e. unaware that consciousness—the inmost—has its origin, as Emerson proclaims, in the voice of the mind. This voice is composed of the voice within—intuition, insights, and the like—plus those enlightened voices of others which we may perceive and embrace. Together, they make up and circumscribe one's consciousness.

I am only trying to emphasize that we waste our time and energy when contesting at the echo or effects level. Nothing is changed for the better when we tackle things "after the fact!" If we would labor effectively, we must get at the root, where causes are set in motion. A brighter reflection—the outmost—depends on brighter lights—the inmost. And this demands nothing less than a greater awareness, an expanding consciousness. To determine the method appropriate to advancing individual liberty, simply reflect on how consciousness is expanded.

EXPANDING ONE'S CONSCIOUSNESS

Expanding consciousness is no simple matter! Indeed, no one can prescribe the technique for another. Our variation—uniqueness—precludes any fixed formula. Among a few rare individuals it appears to come as easily and naturally as physical growth. But for the most of us this growth requires disciplines and exertions so difficult that acceptance and adoption are thwarted. Three generalities, however, apply to everyone: (1) this is a wholly introspective exercise—concentration on the self; (2) it requires a passionate wanting-to-know-it-ness; and (3) it demands integrity, an accurate reflection in word and deed of whatever one's highest conscience dictates as right.

Have I painted a picture too glum to warrant enthusiasm? To the contrary, it is filled with hope. Why this assertion? The future is hopeful because there are in America today more persons than our cause needs who, once aware of the proper method, can and will supply all the inmost required. To prove my point, look in the mirror and behold one of these individuals.

A LONELY VENTURE

Is this too lonely a venture? No, the most delightful companions are those who seek one's light or those from whom light is sought.

Leo Tolstoy lends his support to this thesis. Except for a varied phrasing, his and Emerson's thoughts are the same:

> One free man says frankly what he thinks and feels in the midst of thousands who by their actions and words maintain just the opposite. It might be supposed that the man who has frankly expressed his thought would remain isolated, yet in most cases it happens that all, or the majority, of the others have long thought and felt the same as he, only they have not expressed it. And what yesterday was

the novel opinion of one man becomes today the general opinion of the majority. And as soon as this opinion is established, at once by imperceptible degrees but irresistibly, the conduct of mankind begins to alter.

Emerson's promise has no flaws: "Speak your latent conviction, and it shall be the universal sense; for the inmost in due time becomes the outmost." Thanks for your help, Ralph Waldo Emerson!

27

OFF THE BEATEN TRACK

Ye are the light of the world. A city
that is set on the top of a hill can-
not be hid.

—MATTHEW 5:14

I have long been intrigued by the seeming paradox that the more one knows the more he knows he does not know. This is another way of saying that every gain in knowledge increasingly exposes one to the infinite unknown.

Another aspect of this intriguing paradox: as a person grows in knowledge he is exposed to a new set of friends—and almost certainly faces a dwindling number of old friends. There are many ways to lose friends, of course, but what I am suggesting is that a dwindling audience is *not necessarily* a sign of failure; on the contrary, it may signify personal progress. This is the point I would like to explore.

Ortega presents us with the reality of this problem:

So far as ideas are concerned, meditation on any theme, if *positive and honest,* inevitably separates him who does the meditating from the opinion prevailing around him, from that which . . . can be called "public" or "popular" opinion. Every intellectual effort sets us apart from the commonplace, and leads us by hidden and difficult paths to secluded spots where we find ourselves amid unaccustomed thoughts. These are the results of meditation.[1]

Why dwell on this? A simple reason: if you are on the right track and gaining in knowledge but fail to read these signs aright, you may throw in the sponge simply because listeners are few; you may call it quits just before the dawn. In a word, I hope to present an antidote for discouragement, a way of viewing matters that will help to "keep the chin up." Not only yours, but my own! In the area of our concern, it is easy to mistake success for failure.

Why? Simply because success is often equated with a growing number of adherents, failure with a declining number, as if the quality of ideas and the quantity of better thinkers go hand in hand. We tend to expect that any improvement in ideas will automatically attract a wider audience; whereas, quite the opposite might happen.

NOT A MATTER OF NUMBERS

My thinking in this matter has been stimulated in part by a slight drop in FEE's mailing list over recent months, while at the same time we are told by others that our publications and seminars are better than ever before—and that we must do something to "reach more people."

---

[1]Jose Ortega y Gasset, *What Is Philosophy?*, New York, 1960, p. 15.

Were numbers here and now the sole measure of success, then the recipe would be (1) a point of view consistent with "public" or "popular" opinions; and, (2) charismatic personalities. Examples can be found in the political realm: engaging and energetic copycats of the current consensus putting themselves in the vanguard.

Were ours just a numbers game, then we would attractively proclaim "free enterprise" and loudly decry "socialism." *And let it go at that!* For there are millions paying lip service to freedom and proclaiming opposition to socialism who are anxious to ally themselves with those of similar leanings—so long as the specific aspects of these opposed ways of life are left unexamined. But never, for heaven's sake, go beyond the generalities and attempt a detailed study of these ideologies! To do so assures alienation, a marked dwindling of old friends, perhaps a few new ones.

Our meditations at FEE over the past quarter century have been positive and honest. Even our detractors concede that we have so operated, and with consistency. In the beginning our position was more or less a generalization: in favor of freedom and opposed to socialism and other variants of authoritarianism. But the more we meditated, the more did some commonly accepted practices of "free enterprisers" and "anti-socialists" show up as bearing the seeds of socialism behind the labels. Further, we have never held the results of these meditations to ourselves for fear of giving offense, that is, we have not bowed to expediency.

For instance, some 20 years ago we published *The Tariff Idea,* a critique of protectionism, the case for freedom in transactions. The criticisms we received were severe, and several large corporate supporters dropped FEE then and thereafter. Over the years all of our books and each of nearly 3,000 essays have, in one way or another, affronted the mores, gone counter to the current trends and accepted opinions. This is to say, we have upheld the basic principles of voluntary exchange, private ownership, limited government while, at the same time, challenging those flaws of coercive or governmental intervention parading under the name of free enterprise. Such unaccustomed thoughts are not popular!

TO FIND A BETTER WAY, ONE MUST DEPART THE BEATEN PATH

This is why the serious freedom devotees may not rely on numbers—popular acclaim—as an objective. For the prime requirement of such an objective is to stay on the beaten track, to go along with commonly accepted notions. But must we not abandon the beaten track if we would *find a better one*? To "go along" is to go without prospect of improvement. To play the numbers game is to accept the fallacies that ought to be exposed and displaced.

The soundness of a philosophy cannot be gauged by numbers of followers. In this respect, the philosophy of freedom is similar to religion. True, we can count the financial supporters of the several religions and the church attendees, but these numbers reveal absolutely nothing as to the depth or profundity of religious convictions. Religious faith, so-called, is founded on diverse forces, ranging all the way from fear and superstition to cosmic consciousness. We must note, however, that all of the significant religions have been inspired by some *one* whose purity of thought—meditations, if you will—provided that rich spiritual insight which made possible the awakening of others.

Continuing the analogy, be it noted that each religion was, initially, an affront to "public" and "popular" opinion, a complete break with the mores. Each was born in an environment more or less hostile to its precepts. These initiators of high ethical, moral, and spiritual ideas have, in every instance, presented thoughts unfamiliar to most people at the time.

It is only when we make progress in learning what the ideal is, while standing foursquare therewith in our proclaimed positions, that we aid the cause of freedom. True, we will never fully comprehend the ideal, let alone realize it, but we can everlastingly strive for this purity in thought. Be certain of this: the nearer we come to knowing and upholding the ideal, the greater is the probability that the good society may emerge. Why? Because men can establish the good society only upon what is right and true. Upon that alone, and nothing else!

Fungus may be spawned by a muck heap; but the good society is the emergence and flowering of the best there is in thoughtful meditation. The best flows always from one—the one who comes nearest to being the perfect exemplar. Viewed in this manner, the so-called problems of society break down to a level a person might comprehend. One's duty is not to fall in step with present imperfections but, rather, to strive for his own perfection. Upon whom, then, does the solution depend? Upon the world's most important person: YOU!

28

IS THERE TIME ENOUGH?

*Time is what we want most, but
what alas! we use worst.*

—PENN

Time after time I hear from those distraught by present
trends or appearances. "We are headed for catastrophe,"
they say, "and fast! There is no time for self-enlightenment
which you folks commend. Yours is a slow, laborious approach. We must act now—in *this* moment of time." List this
high among all the notions that do mischief to the advance-
ment of human freedom.

Bear in mind that the free society—no man-concocted restraints against the release of creative energy—is an intellectual, moral, and spiritual attainment. It is structured from
the knowledge and the practice of difficult human virtues.
Freedom's flag is high on the mast only when it is raised
there by wisdom. And it is sustained there only by an endur-
ing and continuing wisdom. Let this vital, sustaining source
falter or weaken and down comes the flag to half-mast—"a
sign of mourning or distress."

185

In politico-economic terms, what is analogous to half-mast? It is authoritarian collectivism or socialism or mercantilism or our own interventionism and welfarism, call it what you will—*a situation fallen into*. Collectivism as a way of life does not represent the triumph of a coherent philosophy; rather it is a manifestation of the abyss into which men sink when not held high by the pursuit of truth and justice. The abandonment of the latter makes inevitable the fire and brimstone of the former. The abyss is not an attainment, as so many misled people proclaim, but a low position brought on by a surrender of ideals or, perhaps we should say, an unwillingness to understand and an inability to explain the miracles wrought by freedom. In a word, the abyss is nothing but a penalty hole for ignorance. Whose ignorance? Everyone who cannot skillfully make the case for freedom! Who can? I am unaware of anyone who has more than scratched the surface.

ACTIVATED IGNORANCE

If we are willing to concede how really ignorant we are when it comes to making the case for freedom, then we may sensibly contemplate what happens when we activate our ignorance, that is, when we put it into high gear. The more we try to sell or peddle—activate—the little we know—"ram it down their necks"—the less will freedom be accepted. Why? Because the fence-straddlers, wondering which way to jump, will think that freedom has no better case than our shallow utterances. They will link freedom to the noisy ignorance and have none of it. Herein lies the fallacy of, "We must act now; time is of the essence." At the root of this fallacy lies a mistaken view of time as related to human beings—or so it seems to me.

We must act here and now, of course. True, there is no time like the present; time is of the essence, and all that. But the question is, how shall I act in *my* time? What can I do that is constructive? How can I best avoid wasting this moment in time that is *mine*?

As a starter, let us acknowledge that raising freedom's flag above half-mast depends on an improving discernment of truth and justice, in a word, on an expanding consciousness. It is possible for me to expand my own consciousness in my own time and this constitutes my problem. I must not, however, confuse my poor understanding at this moment in time with Infinite Consciousness and infinite time. To do so is to be drawn off course, to depart from reality, to regard my minuscule wisdom as God's Omniscience and my fleeting moment as eternity.

True, no one can comprehend Infinite Consciousness or infinite truth or infinite time, but there are many ways one can become aware of infinity. Infinite time is beyond the imagination, but we come to an awareness of it merely by acknowledging that finite time cannot be imagined: a point in time beyond which there is no time. The same with infinite truth: a body of truths beyond which there could be no more truth—unimaginable for finite man![1]

---

[1]Another way to gain awareness: Take the integer 1 and write 1-1-1-1-1-1 on and on. Never will there be a point beyond which another 1 cannot be added. Or divide 1 by 2 and keep on dividing. There never will be a fraction so small but what it is still divisible.

These somewhat esoteric observations about infinity are only for the purpose of emphasizing how I can constructively employ my own earthly moment. If not careful, I will forego my duties in the interest of setting humanity straight—the Creator's role. By so doing, I reject the possible and attempt the impossible.

INDIVIDUAL ACHIEVEMENT

At the human level, no fraction of infinite truth, consciousness, wisdom is possessed except by discrete individuals as they pursue and come into a perception of these qualities. Thus, raising freedom's flag high on the mast rests exclusively on how industriously and conscientiously you and I employ our time. Wise men have recognized and shared their counsel with us. A sampling:

> As every thread of gold is valuable, so is every moment of time.—J. MASON

> If time be of all things the most precious, wasting time must be the greatest prodigality, since lost time is never found again; and what we call time enough always proves little enough.—FRANKLIN

> Make use of time if thou lovest eternity; yesterday cannot be recalled; tomorrow cannot be assured; only today is thine, which if thou procrastinate, thou losest.—QUARLES.

> There is no saying shocks me so much as that which I hear very often, "that a man does not know how to pass his time."—COWLEY

You'll find as you grow older that you weren't born such a very great while ago after all. Time shortens up.—HOWELLS

Regret for time wasted can become a power for good in the time that remains. And the time that remains is time enough, if we will only stop the waste and the idle, the useless regretting.—BRISBANE

Time well employed is Satan's deadliest foe; it leaves no opening for the lurking fiend.—C. WILCOX

As if you could kill time without injuring eternity! —THOREAU

Lost yesterday, somewhere between sunrise and sunset, two golden hours, each set with sixty diamond minutes. No reward is offered, for they are gone forever!—SIGOURNEY

I wasted time, and now doth time waste me.

—SHAKESPEARE

Well arranged time is the surest mark of a well arranged mind.—PITMAN

AM I WASTING TIME?

I ask again, is there time enough? This poses the truly relevant question: Am I employing my own time—fleeting and finite though it be—as diligently and intelligently as possible? For those whose answer is negative there is not time enough, not even in two or twenty lifetimes! But, if affirmative, then my allotted time is spacious enough for me to perform my part in hoisting freedom's flag. The balance of the problem—

the rest of the human situation—is the Lord's; as far as I know, the only part of the world for which He holds me responsible is myself and my use of the time given me.

Self-enlightenment is admittedly difficult; it is generally regarded as too rare an accomplishment to be an effective remedy for social disaster. But how, in heaven's name, can an unenlightened person enlighten someone else! It is impossible! Choose difficulty, therefore; not impossibility!

Far more common, however, is the cry that self-enlightenment is too slow. The laggard we bemoan can be identified by looking in the mirror. This character, whoever he may be, is forever powerless to hasten enlightenment other than his own. In doubt? Then in what other manner can I hasten yours? True, we are in a hurry but choose self-acceleration, the only kind that has any get up and go to it.

Virtues and talents are required to raise freedom's flag from half-mast. Let each lend that which is within his power during his time. As George Washington phrased this idea: "Let us raise a standard to which the wise and honest can repair. The event is in the hand of God."

29

ACTUALLY, WHAT'S THE HURRY?

Wisely and slow; they stumble that
run fast.
—SHAKESPEARE

Even as Emerson, I have never found a language of sufficient energy to convey the importance of integrity and other virtues. Nor have I been able to communicate what I sense to be the distinction between a program for destruction and methods for achieving creative objectives. Attempts to create through destructive actions are doomed to fail. As reason and logic suggest, "the end pre-exists in the means." Employ means appropriate to destructive aims and the result will be destructive—it has to be. Yet, it seems most difficult to establish and explain this point with respect to our own work.

As a starter, contemplate this sample from "The Revolutionary Catechism," the credo followed by Lenin, Stalin, and others, the most revoltingly destructive objective I have ever read:

Night and day he [the revolutionary] must have but one

thought, one aim—merciless destruction. He must hate everyone and everything in it with an equal hatred.[1]

What kind of action is best suited to achieve this mad and destructive objective? Its essence has to be violent confrontation and the elimination or removal of all who stand in the way. This means shooting, clubbing, incarceration, lying, cheating, defamation, name-calling, utter intolerance. The old moral standards and ideals are discarded. There can be no admission of any higher consciousness than the paranoid fanaticism exhibited in these wild, depraved offshoots of the human race. Nothing so low is to be found in the animal world.

NONE IS PERFECT

The above is but the nadir in destructive aims. Careful assessment reveals that this degeneracy exists to some degree in all of us; there are few, if any, in whom no traces of these faults exist. Who among us is simon-pure? Have I entirely freed myself of this destructive attitude? Determining how much of this depravity is to be found among Americans is easy enough: merely assay our own political front with its rapidly growing and popularly supported authoritarianism— "do as I say, or else." For the past forty years elections have been races between political parties each sparked by the very domineering traits we profess to abhor in others.

True, we have not stooped to shooting political opponents,

---

[1]See "The Revolutionary Catechism," written by Nechayev, in *The Life and Death of Lenin* by Robert Payne, New York, 1964, pp. 24-29.

but the recent rash of bombings and assassinations is sympto-
matic. Our own destructive aims are numerous enough that
we may deduce the type of action forthcoming for their attainment. We need not turn to revolutionary handbooks for
such instruction.

The password for destructive ends is "hurry." Don't think!
Lie, pin a bad label on dissenters—right now! Power grab-
bing admits of no scruples. It is a game of rapid-fire confrontation, the speedier the better. Strike first or get struck, as in
a prize fight. Merely observe the military tactics and ter-
minology associated with the numerous domestic welfare
programs. Appeals to force rather than reason!

CONFRONTATION!

In any event, our own destructive aims are so prevalent—
along with the means or tactics appropriate for their attainment—that, thoughtlessly, most people resort to these very
same means to achieve creative ends. Discouragingly typical
are these words from a thoroughgoing anti-socialist:

> I believe it is my duty and your duty to *fight* these sub-
> versive organizations with everything we have. If you do
> not wish to defend America other than to explain the ad-
> vantages of private enterprise, then I must with disap-
> pointment and sorrow say farewell to FEE.

In a word, confrontation! What is meant by *fight*? Surely
not shooting! Were that the case, Nechayev's Catechism
could be used word for word. Only the title would need to
be changed to "A Reactionary's Catechism."

How are we to break ourselves of this pernicious habit? That is the question. Doubtless, our friend who sends his farewell would scrupulously avoid the tactic of confrontation if he knew that it would aid and abet a way of life he abhors. However, he does not know; and for two reasons: (1) he does not understand that this is a mind-changing problem, and (2) he does not see that his proposed action would induce a reaction featured not by correction but by a proliferation of the ways he would be rid of. Call a sinner a devil and he will not thereby become saintly but will only be hardened in his sins. If I call you a so-and-so, you will not be attracted to but repulsed by my point of view. The sum of it is that people are not pushed, shoved, forced, bashed into virtue. Confrontation in any of its forms is virtue's antagonist; it is a tactic appropriate only to destructive aims.

CHOOSING THE MEANS

I wish as much as anyone to be rid of coercive collectivism in all its forms—call it socialism, communism, or whatever. But I must carefully assess the means proposed for doing this lest I aggravate rather than improve the situation. At the very least, I must employ only those means which are appropriate to creative ends, for increasing human liberty is unquestionably in the creative realm.

Coercive collectivism grows so rapidly in this and other countries because there are so few who understand and can explain with clarity its opposite: namely, the free market, private ownership, limited government way of life along with its moral and spiritual antecedents. Count the ones known to you personally who can do more than rant and sputter at the nonsense. How many are skilled expositors of the freedom philosophy?

The absence of an understanding of freedom amounts to an intellectual vacuum into which all sorts of collectivist ideas flow. Nonsense has no choice except to follow the lines of least resistance; it has to obey its nature and, thus, flows willy-nilly into empty heads.

The task, then, is to get an ever-improving understanding into our own heads. If this point be granted, we are faced with an endeavor that is exclusively creative: learning, thinking in areas yet unexplored, philosophizing.

Reflect on what this means. Such an endeavor is featured not only by study and deep thought but by reflection and an "ability to see and understand clearly the inner nature of things": insight. These qualities of the soul and mind can never be hurried. What could be more absurd than to exclaim: "I am now going to have some brilliant ideas and great insights!" These qualities do not respond to commands or incantations.

INHIBITIONS TO CREATIVITY

No one can accurately formulate the conditions congenial to creativity, even for self, let alone for others. The best one can do is to identify and then abandon those postures and attitudes which inhibit creativity. Here are a few that occur to me.

- Haste: except to get day-to-day chores into the past tense and thus to free oneself for reflection, impatience is a posture unfavorable to new ideas and insights. These cannot be rushed into mind; rather, they flow best into a mind that is at peace with itself. While the world around us with all of its shocking appearances seems to demand action now, that is a demand that cannot be met. Why? It is contrary to the way monumental shifts in understanding are brought about. Therefore, think not in terms of any immediate effects, but of the long range consequences when people come to new perceptions of truth. A great genius' new light is rarely beheld in the day of its advent. More than likely months, years, decades, or even centuries will pass before many take sight of it. Let not this fact of life disturb one's reflections.

- Confrontation: growth in awareness, perception, consciousness never occurs while berating others orally or physically. Violence is an affliction, and it is highly contagious.

- Anger: no creative act was ever done in anger. One never reflects or thinks when thus impassioned.

- Hate is dark as love is light. Insight cannot penetrate the darkness of hatred.

- Worry: fret not over that which is beyond your control. This allows unfettered attention to self-improvement, which is the limit of any person's responsibility.

In summary, our problem is one of achieving an about-face in thinking, a switch from destructive aims and methods to an enlightenment. We need only bear in mind that the desired change depends upon the law of attraction: others will turn to you or me if, in *their* judgment, we have light they wish to share.

If we would rise above the squabbles and the conflicts with their destructive results, we must see how much candle power of our own we can generate. My counsel to concerned individuals is to stay out of the fight and get into the game; either brighten up or forget the whole thing. There is fun in making the first choice—serious but sportive—and in it lies the only hope for freedom.

30

FINDING OUT

If I have ever made any valuable discoveries, it has been owing more to patient attention, than to any other talent.

—SIR ISAAC NEWTON

The social problems of our time which so gravely concern freedom devotees can never be resolved by our singling out and scolding those presumed responsible. We may derive satisfaction from "telling 'em off," but this solves nothing. The correct procedure is quite the opposite: it requires *finding out* on your part as well as mine. This is to say that the more a person increases his awareness, the more will others try to "find out" from him. The "telling 'em off" approach—trying to ram one's "wisdom" into their "stupid" heads—only darkens the way to understanding. Mere disparagement tends to convince people that their fallacies must be right; it never enlightens. Why? The method itself is the height of folly, being wholly at odds with the finding-out or listening or discovering process.

In the opening chapter I referred to the Voices Without and the Voice Within—listening to each, finding out from both. I voiced the opinion that "all the truth and righteousness known to man originates as the Voice Within." Among the required disciplines: *Concentration—prepare to think it through*! This is the essence of an interesting theory I came upon years ago.

If my theory is correct, the frequency of ideas *per* minute, so to speak, will be greatly increased under a powerful mood of concentration. Under these conditions the mind of the artist [poet, painter, philosopher, musician, or who-ever] becomes, as it were, an intense magnetic field gathering up ideas from realms of mind not possible to contact under ordinary circumstances.[1]

The term, "magnetic field," is as descriptive of this phenomenon as any I have come upon; the theory is that inspiration responds *as if* the mind in focus attracts ideas to itself. There is at work at the human level what a distinguished scientist refers to as "this mysterious attractive force."

All the phenomena of astronomy, which had baffled the acutest minds since the dawn of history, the movement of the heavens, of the sun and the moon, the very complex movement of the planets, suddenly tumble together and become intelligible in terms of the one staggering assumption, this mysterious "attractive force."[2]

---

[1]Rosamond E. M. Harding, *The Anatomy of Inspiration,* Cambridge, England, 1967, p. 135.

[2]Anthony Standen, *Science As A Sacred Cow,* New York, 1950, pp. 63-64.

STICK TO COMMON SENSE

Let Galileo make my concluding point as he explains why he wrote his theories in what he called "the colloquial tongue":

> I am induced to do this by seeing how young men are sent through the universities at random to be made physicians, philosophers, and so on; thus many of them are committed to professions for which they are unsuited, while other men who would be fitted for these are taken up by family cares and other occupations remote from literature. The latter are, as Ruzzante would say, furnished with "horse sense," but because they are unable to read things that are "Greek to them" they become convinced that in those "big books there are great things of logic and philosophy and still more that is way over their heads." *Now I want them to see that just as nature has given to them, as well as to philosophers, eyes with which to see her works, so she has also given them brains capable of penetrating and understanding them.*[3] (Italics added)

What instruction emerges? It is that you—whoever you are, whatever your status, however much or little your formal schooling—never, never sell yourself short. Remember Dr. Fritz Kunkel's astute observation: "Immense hidden powers lurk in the unconscious of the most common man—indeed, of all people without exception." My experience during the past forty years confirms this, which is to say, that some of the finest thinking I have encountered—creativity—has emerged

---

[3]See *Discoveries and Opinions of Galileo,* Translated by Stillman Drake, Garden City, N.Y., 1957, p. 84.

as much from so-called commoners as from the acclaimed elite.

Finding out what these hidden powers are—unmasking, listening to the Voice Within—should be the aim of anyone and everyone. The reward? Readiness!

INDEX

Prepared by Vernelia A. Crawford

The letter "n" following a number indicates a footnote.

203